Locality

Linguistic Inquiry Monographs
Samuel Jay Keyser, general editor

Locality: Maria Rita Manzini

A Theory and Some of Its
Empirical Consequences

The MIT Press
Cambridge, Massachusetts
London, England

This book was set in Times Roman by Asco Trade Typesetting Ltd., Hong Kong, and was printed and bound in the United States of America.

Library of Congress Cataloging-in-Publication Data

Manzini, Maria Rita.
   Locality: a theory and some of its empirical consequences / Maria Rita Manzini.
      p.   cm.—(Linguistic inquiry monographs; 19)
   Includes bibliographical references (p.   ) and index.
   ISBN 0-262-13279-6 (hc).—ISBN 0-262-63140-7 (pbk)
   1. Generative grammar. I. Title. II. Series.
P158.M35   1992
415—dc20   91-43205
                                                              CIP

To my family

Contents

Series Foreword

We are pleased to present this monograph as the nineteenth in the series *Linguistic Inquiry Monographs*. These monographs will present new and original research beyond the scope of the article, and we hope they will benefit our field by bringing to it perspectives that will stimulate further research and insight.

Originally published in limited edition, the *Linguistic Inquiry Monograph* series is now available on a much wider scale. This change is due to the great interest engendered by the series and the needs of a growing readership. The editors wish to thank the readers for their support and welcome suggestions about future directions the series might take.

Samuel Jay Keyser
for the Editorial Board

Acknowledgments

I started the work that eventually led to this book when *Barriers* (Chomsky 1986a) was first circulated. Because of his contribution to the field, and because of his role as my teacher while I studied at MIT, Noam Chomsky has greatly influenced this book, and indeed all of my work. It is only fitting, then, that he should be remembered at the beginning.

I presented early installments of *Locality* at four successive GLOW conferences, in Barcelona (1986), Venice (1987), Budapest (1988), and Cambridge (1990), and partial or preliminary reports of its proposals are found in Manzini 1988, 1990, to appear b. A number of my publications concerning binding theory (in particular, Manzini 1991a, 1991b, to appear a) are related directly or indirectly to the topics discussed here. They correspond to papers presented at conferences and colloquia at the University of Groningen (1987), Essex University (1987), and the CNRS (Paris, 1990). The organizers and audiences at those sites, as well as at MIT (1986), the University of Paris VII (1987), the Linguistic Association of Great Britain's conferences at Durham University (1988) and Manchester University (1989), the Irvine Conference on Subjects (1989), the Incontro di Grammatica Generativa (Pisa, 1990), the Groningen/NIAS Talks (1990), the University of Utrecht (1990), and the University of Florence (1991) are hereby warmly acknowledged. I also greatly benefited from graduate courses I taught at SOAS (London) and at Oxford University; my thanks to R. Kempson and A. Davies for their kind invitations.

During part of the period when the manuscript was being prepared I served as a lecturer in the Department of Italian at University College London. I must express here my appreciation to L. Lepschy, my Head of Department, for allowing me as much scope for pure research as was compatible with the department's work. I am also very grateful to the Departments of Linguistics at University College, to which I am presently attached, and at SOAS, for making me feel welcome in the London linguistic community. In (greater) London I would like to thank in particular M. Brody, N. Smith, H. van de Koot, D. Wilson, R. Carston, R. Kempson, W. Chao, A. Cormack, G. Lepschy, as well as H. Borer, a sometimes visitor.

The last draft but one of this work was prepared at the Netherlands Institute for Advanced Studies (NIAS), where I spent a semester as a Resident Scholar as part of the research group on The Logical Problem of Language Acquisition coordinated by T. Hoekstra and H. van der Hulst of the University of Leiden. For their intellectual companionship I am grateful to the other members of the group, especially T. Borowsky and Ch. Koster.

I am indebted to L. Rizzi for a detailed review of the first version of the book. T. Taraldsen examined the proposals in Manzini 1988 in his graduate-level class. J.-R. Vergnaud inspired my use of the term *address* and much more importantly its conception. T. Hoekstra suggested that my original explanation of the Complex NP Constraint could be extended to include Tense and definiteness islands. M. Brody prodded me on the topic of referentiality. Of the many conversations with people working on closely related hypotheses, I would particularly like to acknowledge those with G. Cinque, J. Frampton, J. Huang, D. Pesetsky, and A. Szabolcsi. Sincere thanks go to the MIT Press and to the anonymous reviewers, especially to the reviewer who followed the manuscript through two successive revisions. Very special thanks to my copyeditor, A. Mark, who made important contributions to the final form of this book.

Finally, I would like to remember the generous friendship extended to me by O. Jaeggli, who sadly is no longer alive to read this.

Introduction

The core proposal of this book is a unified theory of locality that subsumes all three major locality principles invoked in current theories, namely, Subjacency, the Empty Category Principle (ECP), and binding theory. The core argument in favor of the locality principle proposed in chapter 2 comes from a set of islands that remain refractory to other treatments, including (complex) NP islands, Tense islands, definiteness islands, and multiple *wh*-islands.

The structure of the book is as follows. Chapter 1 lays out the empirical problem and gives an overview of the proposed solution. It also provides an introduction to the three main alternatives to the theory proposed here, namely, the barriers approach (Chomsky 1986a), the antecedent-based approach (Aoun 1985; Rizzi 1990), and the connectedness approach (Kayne 1983; Pesetsky 1982). Chapter 2 contains a step-by-step presentation of my theory, including a unification of the disjunction between Subjacency and the antecedent government clause of the ECP, and a unification of the ECP-internal disjunction between the antecedent government clause and the head government clause.

Chapter 3 centers on the empirical side of the proposal. It argues that complex NP islands, Tense islands, and definiteness islands all belong to the same fundamental type characterized by the presence of a denotational head, N, T, or D, whereas multiple *wh*-islands reflect the fact that at most two overlapping extraction paths are available at any given point in a derivation. The claim that my theory is empirically superior crucially rests on its ability to predict these data. Chapter 4 completes the discussion by taking binding into account. Under my theory, the same locality principle that accounts for movement also accounts for binding, but without any need for anaphors to move at any level of representation.

I would like to stress that this book is not meant as an encyclopedia of the grammatical principles and phenomena mentioned so far. Nor is its existence justified by the discovery of some new type of data and/or by the systematization of some previously unanalyzed language. Rather, the goal of the book is to organize the considerable mass of evidence now extant on local dependencies according to what I believe to be genuinely novel principles. Its main justification is that the proposals it advances, which in turn represent a simplification of other available analyses, place some of the most poorly understood evidence in the literature within a theoretical framework.

The chapters in the book differ somewhat in character. Chapter 1 is meant to provide accessible terms of reference for the ensuing debate. Though the perspective is admittedly biased, it is so in one respect only, namely, in that the crucial property of each theory examined is taken to be the extent to which it does or does not allow for unification. Thus, it could easily be used as (part of) a graduate introduction to locality theory. Chapter 2 presents the core statement of my theory, developing it step by step from previous models in the literature.

Chapter 3 represents the more open-ended side of the enterprise. It delves into various sets of data that either have been used to support alternative theories or on the contrary remain mysterious under such theories. Finally, in its central concern for a basic statement of the theory, chapter 4 is essentially a continuation of chapter 2, concerning locality conditions on anaphors and pronouns rather than on movement.

Chapter 1
The Locality Problem

1.1 The Theoretical Problem and Some Residual Empirical Ones

Two types of grammatical dependencies can be distinguished according to the locality constraints they are subject to. The first type is characterized by strict locality conditions. These "bounded" dependencies include (for instance) anaphoric relations with reflexives and reciprocals, and their mirror image, disjoint reference relations with pronouns. Thus, the well-formed anaphoric dependency in (1), which does not cross a sentence boundary, contrasts with the ill-formed dependency in (2), which does. Conversely, disjoint reference with a pronoun is enforced internally to a sentence, as in (3), but not across a sentence boundary, as in (4).

(1) John$_i$ likes himself$_i$

(2) *John$_i$ thinks that [Mary likes himself$_i$]

(3) *John$_i$ likes him$_i$

(4) John$_i$ thinks that [Mary likes him$_i$]

A second type of dependency that displays a strict locality behavior is A-movement. Thus, raising is allowed from an embedded subject to an immediately superordinate subject, as in (5) and (6); and successive applications of raising, as in (7), also produce well-formed results. But long-distance raising, crossing an intermediate subject, as in (8), is ill formed.

(5) John$_i$ appears [t$_i$ to win]

(6) John$_i$ is likely [t$_i$ to win]

(7) John$_i$ appears [t$_i$ to be likely [t$_i$ to win]]

(8) *John$_i$ appears that [it is likely [t$_i$ to win]]

Examples like those in (1)–(8) and a discussion of their theoretical significance are found in Chomsky 1973. A third type of strictly local dependency, distinguished more recently, is head movement. Thus, we assume that a sentence like (9) includes a C(omplementizer) head, represented by *if*, an I(nflection) head, represented by the modal *will*, and a number of V heads, represented by the auxiliary *have* and by *finished*.

(9) ... if [Bill will [have [finished his work]]]

In the absence of a modal it can be argued, as does Pollock (1989a), that the auxiliary must move to I, in order to provide a realization for the inflectional material, as in (10).

(10) ... if [Bill has$_i$ [t$_i$ [finished his work]]]

Furthermore, in a main sentence, a modal or an auxiliary must move to C in order for a question to be formed (say, for the reason detailed by Rizzi (1991)), as in (11)–(12).

(11) Will$_i$ [Bill t$_i$ [have [finished his work]]]

(12) Has$_i$ [Bill t$_i$ [t$_i$ [finished his work]]]

But suppose an auxiliary is moved to C from its original V position, bypassing I as in (13), where I is already filled by a modal; the result is ungrammatical.

(13) *Have$_i$ [Bill will [t$_i$ [finished his work]]]

The descriptive generalization corresponding to the paradigm (10)–(13) is Travis's (1984) Head Movement Constraint, which states that movement is only possible from a head position to the immediately superordinate one. Thus, strict locality is again observed.

Contrasting with the dependencies in (1)–(13) is a class of grammatical dependencies that appear to be "unbounded," in that the two members of the dependency can occur an indefinite distance apart. A typical example is the sort of $\bar{\text{A}}$-movement shown in (14)–(16); and one can imagine examples in which the distance between the *wh*-phrase and its trace, measured for instance in terms of sentence boundaries crossed, is even greater.

(14) Who$_i$ do you like t$_i$

(15) Who$_i$ do you believe [Peter likes t$_i$]

(16) Who$_i$ do you believe [Peter said [that Mary likes t$_i$]]

As is well known, there is evidence, going back to Ross (1967), that this type of dependency is itself severely constrained. Thus, $\bar{\text{A}}$-movement out of a subject, as in (17), out of an adjunct, as in (18), or out of a relative clause, as in (19), is ill formed, regardless of the total distance (again measured, for instance, in terms of sentence boundaries crossed) between the *wh*-phrase and its trace.

(17) *What$_i$ does [explaining t$_i$] bother you

(18) *What$_i$ was Mary bothered [because Peter explained t$_i$]

(19) *What$_i$ do you know the girl [that explained t$_i$]

Nevertheless, though *wh*-dependencies are subject to locality constraints in the form of islands, as in (17)–(19), contrasts like the ones between (2) and (15) and between (8) and (15) remain to be explained.

The situation is further complicated by the contrast discovered by Huang (1982) between the locality behavior of $\bar{A}$-dependencies created by arguments, such as those in (14)–(19), and that of $\bar{A}$-dependencies created by adjuncts, such as *how* or *why*. Thus, extracting an argument out of a sentence introduced by a *wh*-phrase produces an interpretable sentence, as in (20), whereas extracting *how* does not, as in (21). The Italian counterpart (22) of the English sentence (20) is perfectly good, as first noted by Rizzi (1980); but the Italian sentence (23), like its English counterpart (21), is uninterpretable.

(20)   What$_i$ do you wonder [how$_j$ to fix t$_i$ t$_j$]

(21) *How$_i$ do you wonder [what$_j$ to fix t$_j$ t$_i$]

(22)   Cosa$_i$ ti chiedi [come$_j$ aggiustare t$_i$ t$_j$]

(23) *Come$_i$ ti chiedi [cosa$_j$ aggiustare t$_i$ t$_j$]

Nevertheless, configurations like (14)–(16), where apparently unbounded *wh*-extraction of arguments is possible, also allow apparently unbounded extraction of adjuncts, as in (24)–(26).

(24) How$_i$ do you fix it t$_i$

(25) How$_i$ do you believe [Peter fixes it t$_i$]

(26) How$_i$ do you believe [Peter said that [Mary fixes it t$_i$]]

Suppose we assume with Aoun (1985) and Rizzi (1990), among others, that $\bar{A}$-dependencies involving arguments, as in (14)–(16), and only those, are in fact unbounded, in the sense that movement can take place in one step over an arbitrary number of sentence boundaries. By contrast, suppose that, as proposed by Chomsky (1973), the unboundedness of

$\bar{\text{A}}$-dependencies involving adjuncts, as in (24)–(26), is only apparent. The adjunct moves in strictly local fashion, stopping in the initial position of each sentence, which is independently known to host *wh*-phrases; in other words, (25) and (26) have derivations like (27) and (28).

(27) How$_i$ do [you believe [t$_i$ [Peter fixed it t$_i$]]]

(28) How$_i$ do [you believe [t$_i$ [Peter said [t$_i$ that [Mary fixes it t$_i$]]]]]

Under these assumptions, the contrast between (20) and (21) becomes transparent. In (20) the argument *wh*-phrase can indeed move in one step, as indicated. But in (21) the adjunct *wh*-phrase ought to move first to the position that is already occupied by *what*. Since the presence of *what* makes this movement impossible, we correctly predict that (21) will be ill formed.

To sum up: If the preceding observations are correct, there are at least four types of grammatical dependencies that display strictly local behavior: anaphora, A-movement, head movement, and $\bar{\text{A}}$-movement of adjuncts. There is also at least one type of dependency that does not display strictly local behavior, namely, $\bar{\text{A}}$-movement of arguments (though this type of dependency too is subject to locality constraints in the form of islands, as in (17)–(19)). To complete the picture, strictly local dependencies are also subject to islands, as illustrated with *wh*-extraction of adjuncts in (29)–(31).

(29) *How$_i$ did [fixing it t$_i$] bother Mary

(30) *How$_i$ was Mary bothered [because John had fixed it t$_i$]

(31) *How$_i$ do you know the girl [that fixed it t$_i$]

We are now in a position to formulate the question that this book addresses. Of course, each of the five above-mentioned dependencies can simply be listed along with its particular locality behavior, as in the previous paragraph. But can a unified account of these behaviors be given? All current theories achieve partial unification. What I propose to show here is that complete unification is possible.

Current theories identify two classes of configurations across which a local dependency cannot be formed. The first corresponds to islands of the type shown in (17)–(19) and (29)–(31), which appear to be entirely insensitive to the nature of the elements involved. In essence, according to Huang's (1982) classification, dependencies that cross object boundaries are allowed, as in (14)–(16) and (24)–(26), but not dependencies that cross subject boundaries, as in (17) and (29), or dependencies that cross adjunct boundaries, as in (18)–(19) and (30)–(31), where the relative clause in (19) and (31) can be assimilated to an adjunct.

The second type of island that current theories identify appears to be crucially sensitive to the nature of the elements involved in dependencies. Thus, heads cannot form dependencies across other heads, as in (13) versus (10)–(12), and adjunct *wh*-phrases cannot form dependencies across other *wh*-phrases, as in (21) versus (24)–(26). More generally, following Rizzi (1990), an element cannot form a dependency across a potential antecedent, thus accounting for the contrasts between (1) and (2) and between (4)–(7) and (8) as well. Of course, in the contrast between (3) and (4) the ability of the pronoun to form a dependency only across a potential antecedent is involved. Argument *wh*-phrases constitute an important exception to this type of behavior, however, in that they are insensitive to antecedent islands, as in (20).

One of the immediate aims of this book is to provide a theory under which the difference with respect to antecedent islands between $\bar{\text{A}}$-dependencies involving arguments and other dependencies does not need to be stipulated—in other words, to eliminate the disjunction between antecedent government and head government in Chomsky's (1981) ECP. The theoretical reasons for seeking nondisjunctive locality principles are evident. Such principles will yield a simpler grammar, where simpler can be understood as more highly modular and/or richer in deductive structure. If they are not simply a notational variant of other theories, then they will also have empirical motivation—in other words, they will be able to predict some new set of behaviors.

Indeed, there are a number of known island behaviors that cannot (immediately) be classified as belonging to either type of island illustrated in (1)–(31). Thus, $\bar{\text{A}}$-movement of an argument is well formed across a single nominal boundary, as in (32), but ill formed across adjacent nominal and sentential boundaries, as in (33), even if the sentence is an argument of N.

(32) Who$_i$ did you see [many portraits of t$_i$]

(33) *Who$_i$ did you see [many attempts [to portray t$_i$]]

Since no adjunct or subject configuration is involved in (33), and no other *wh*-element is present, neither currently distinguished type of island subsumes the island in (33), at least without further stipulation.

As before, the situation is complicated by the asymmetry in the behavior of arguments and adjuncts under extraction. Thus, an adjunct cannot even be extracted across a single nominal boundary, as in (34).

(34) *[With what kind of sleeves]$_i$ did you see [many sweaters t$_i$]

Again, this deviates from the characterization of both classes of islands illustrated in (1)–(31). (33)–(34) instead appear to require some stipulation about extractability across N heads, as opposed to V heads.

Similarly, if Chomsky (1986a) is correct, whether or not a *wh*-dependency is well formed across a *wh*-island depends on the presence or absence of Tense in the island. Thus, by contrast with (20), (35) is ill formed.

(35) *What$_i$ did you wonder [how I repaired t$_i$]

Again, object configurations are involved throughout; furthermore, *wh*-dependencies involving arguments are not sensitive to *wh*-antecedents. Hence, the island in (35) appears to be irreducible to either of the two well-understood types.

Finally, although Ā-dependencies can be created across a single nominal boundary, as in (32), their acceptability depends on the nominal being indefinite. The presence of a definite determiner creates an island, as in (36).

(36) *Who$_i$ did you see [the many portraits of t$_i$]

Again, the contrast cannot be explained in terms of object versus subject or adjunct configurations, or in terms of the presence of other *wh*-elements.

As pointed out by T. Hoekstra (personal communication), all of the islands in (33)–(36) can be seen as belonging to a single type, which involves the presence of a head with denoting properties of some sort: an N head in (33)–(34), a T head in (35), and a definite D head in (36). The first major empirical argument in favor of the theory proposed here will be that it allows the islands in (33)–(36) to be distinguished as a coherent class, and eventually to be derived.

Overlapping *wh*-dependencies constitute another island behavior that current theories cannot explain. Thus, *wh*-movement of an argument across another *wh*-element is well formed, as in (20). But if a third *wh*-element, again an argument, is moved, creating a triple extraction, the resulting sentence is ungrammatical, as in (37).

(37) *[Which books]$_i$ did you wonder [to which student]$_j$ to ask [whether to give t$_i$ t$_j$]

The second major empirical argument in favor of the theory proposed here will be that it correctly predicts that no more than two Ā-dependencies can coexist in any given portion of a tree, thus automatically excluding (37).

To see that the two types of islands in (33)–(36) and (37) interact, it is sufficient to consider what happens when more than one argument of N, rather than of V, is *wh*-moved. In Italian, if not in English, both (38) and (39), where two different arguments of N are *wh*-moved one at a time, are fundamentally well formed.

(38) [Di che pittore]$_i$ hai visto [un ritratto di Aristotele t$_i$]
of which painter have you seen a portrait of Aristotle

(39) [Di che filosofo]$_i$ hai visto [un ritratto t$_i$ di Rembrandt]
of which philosopher have you seen a portrait of Rembrandt

However, if both arguments are *wh*-moved at once, as in (40), the resulting sentence is as unacceptable as (37).

(40) *[Di che pittore]$_i$ ti chiedi [di che filosofo]$_j$ comprare
of which painter do you wonder of which philosopher to buy
[un ritratto t$_j$ t$_i$]
a portrait

Thus, it appears that the presence of an N decreases the available *wh*-movement paths from two to one. This prediction also follows from the theory proposed here, as desired.

In brief, the general theoretical problem that we will be addressing is to unify the various locality conditions on grammatical dependencies. This is essentially a simplicity problem, or a problem in maximizing the modularity and/or deductive depth of the model. The empirical problems that we will address at the same time are the head islands in (33)–(36) and the multiple extraction islands in (37) and (40). I will claim that the theoretical problem and the empirical ones admit of one and the same solution.

1.2 The Barriers Solution

As a preliminary step, I will introduce some major current theories of locality, beginning with Chomsky's (1986a) barriers theory. According to Chomsky the canonical structure of a sentence includes two functional heads, I and C, in addition to the lexical head V, as in (41) (where the subject position is identified with the Spec of IP position).

(41)

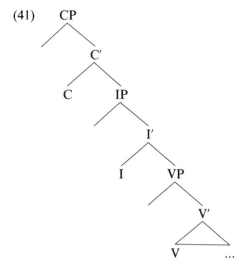

The theory of Subjacency is based on the notion of L-marking, which in turn is based on the notion of θ-government. θ-government is θ-marking by a head, as in (42). L-marking is θ-government by a lexical category, as in (43).

(42) β θ-governs α iff β is a head, β θ-marks α, and β is a sister to α.

(43) β L-marks α iff β is lexical and β θ-governs α.

Subjacency is then defined in terms of the notion of barrier. A maximal projection that dominates a given category can be a barrier for it, inherently or by inheritance. It is inherently a barrier if it is not L-marked (i.e., in Chomsky's (1986a) terms, if it is a blocking category (BC)); it is a barrier by inheritance if it is the first maximal projection that dominates a BC. IP, however, is an exception. It can be a barrier by inheritance, and barrierhood can be inherited from it; but it cannot be an inherent barrier. The relevant definitions are as follows:

(44) β is a BC for α iff β is an XP, β dominates α, and β is not L-marked.

(45) β is a barrier for α iff β (other than IP) is a BC for α, or β is the first XP that dominates a BC for α.

Crucially, although the notion of barrier is defined in terms of dominance, Subjacency itself is stated in terms of exclusion, where dominance is defined as in (46), following May (1985), and exclusion is defined as in (47).

(46) β dominates α only if all segments of β dominate α.

(47) β excludes α iff no segments of β dominate α.

The interplay of dominance and exclusion has the effect of making any adjunction to a maximal projection into an escape hatch. However, adjunction to two maximal projections, CP and NP, is blocked by a constraint against adjunction to an argument. Furthermore, IP is exceptional in that nothing may be adjoined to it. (48) expresses these restrictions.

(48) Arguments and IPs cannot be adjoined to.

Under Subjacency no category can cross more than one barrier (i.e., no more than one barrier for the position moved from can exclude the position moved into); hence, Subjacency is violated if two or more barriers are crossed, as in (49).

(49) *Subjacency*
    If α is a trace, there is an antecedent β for α such that at most one barrier for α excludes β.

The theory in (41)–(49) predicts three fundamental types of islands: subject islands, adjunct islands, and complex NP islands involving relative clauses. Consider first a typical subject island violation, as in (17), repeated here; the structure associated with it is (50).

(17) *What$_i$ does [explaining t$_i$] bother you

(50)

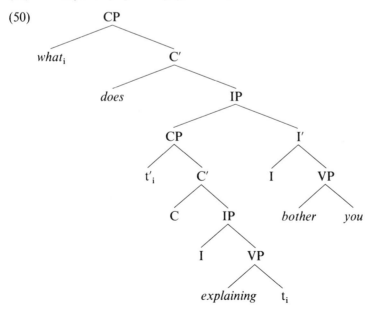

Here we assume that the *wh*-phrase being extracted can successfully move from t to t'. Its next possible landing site is the Spec of the matrix CP; but this movement crosses two barriers. The embedded CP is of course a BC and a barrier for t' since it is not θ-governed by a lexical head and hence is not L-marked; the matrix IP is a barrier for t' by inheritance, because it is the first maximal projection that dominates CP. Thus, the final movement violates Subjacency, and the ungrammaticality of (17) is correctly predicted.

Similar considerations apply in the case of adjunct islands. A relevant example is (18), repeated here; its corresponding structure is (51), where again we assume that the *wh*-phrase being extracted can successfully reach the position of t'.

(18) *What$_i$ was Mary bothered [because Peter explained t$_i$]

(51)

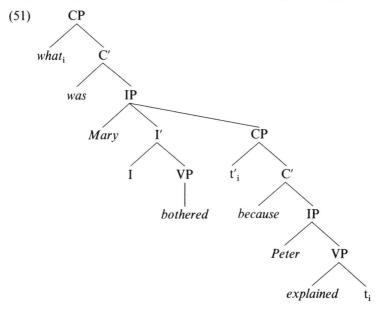

Following Chomsky (1986a), in (51) we assume that adjuncts are generated as sisters of I'. If so, it is obvious that the embedded CP in (51) is a BC and a barrier for t' because it is not L-marked; at the same time the matrix IP is a barrier for t' by inheritance from CP. Hence, movement from t' to the next possible landing site—namely, the Spec of the matrix CP—crosses two barriers and violates Subjacency.

Finally, complex NP island violations, which are illustrated by examples like (19), repeated here, are predicted on the basis of a structure like (52).

(19) *What$_i$ do you know the girl [that explained t$_i$]

(52)

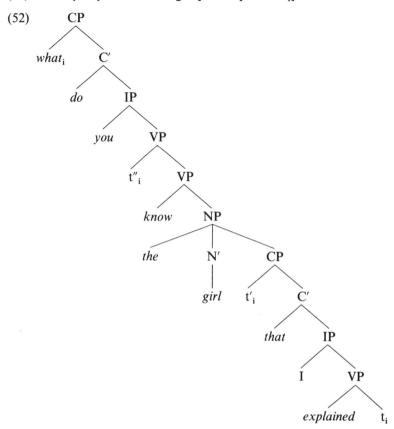

In (52) the relative clause is a sister of N', and we assume as usual that the *wh*-phrase can successfully reach the *t'* position. The embedded CP is of course a BC and a barrier for *t'* because it is not L-marked, and NP is a barrier by inheritance from CP. In this case the next possible landing site for the *wh*-phrase is a VP-adjoined position, *t"*; since two barriers are crossed from *t'* to *t"*, Subjacency is again violated.

Now consider then the ECP. Chomsky's (1986a) version of the ECP states that a trace must either be θ-governed or governed by an antecedent, as in (53).

(53) *ECP*
If α is a trace
a. α is θ-governed; or
b. there is an antecedent β for α such that β governs α.

θ-government has already been defined in (42); government on the other hand is defined to hold between a category and its antecedent just in case no barriers intervene between them, as in (54).

(54) β governs α iff there is no barrier for α that excludes β.

Hence, government does not hold and the ECP is violated when an (antecedent, trace) link crosses one barrier. Since the notion of barrier relevant for Subjacency is also relevant for the ECP, Subjacency and (the antecedent government clause of) the ECP differ in that an ECP violation is defined in terms of crossing just one barrier, whereas a Subjacency violation is defined in terms of crossing two or more.

Objects, which are clearly θ-marked by a head and therefore θ-governed, always satisfy the ECP under the θ-government clause; hence, they do not need to satisfy the antecedent government clause. Adjuncts, on the other hand, which do not satisfy the θ-government clause of the ECP and must therefore satisfy the antecedent government clause, display more restrictive locality patterns than direct objects. In particular, in addition to Subjacency violations like (50)–(52), adjuncts give rise to (strong) *wh*-island violations like (21), repeated here. The relevant structure for such violations is provided in (55).

(21) *How$_i$ do you wonder [what$_j$ to fix t$_j$ t$_i$]

(55)

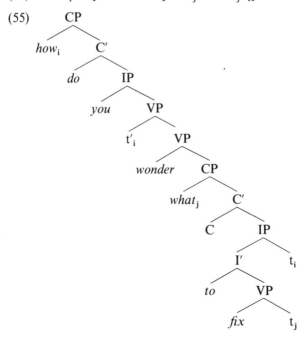

t_i in (55) represents the base-generated position of the adjunct, on the assumption that an adjunct is a daughter of IP, much as in (51). The embedded IP is of course a BC since it is not L-marked; but it is not a(n inherent) barrier for t_i. Hence, if the adjunct can move to the embedded Spec of CP position, no violation ensues, accounting for the well-formedness of long-distance adjunct extractions in the absence of *wh*-islands, as in (25) (*How$_i$ do you believe Peter fixes it t_i*). If the Spec of CP position is filled, however, a barrier is crossed. Indeed, the embedded CP, which is the first maximal projection that dominates IP, is a barrier for t_i by inheritance. Thus, when the adjunct crosses the CP barrier to reach its next possible landing site, the VP-adjoined position t'_i, it violates the antecedent government clause of the ECP, correctly predicting the ill-formedness of (21). On the other hand, if the extracted element is θ-governed, then in the absence of any antecedent government requirement the resulting sentence is predicted to be well formed, correctly accounting for the (relative) acceptability of *wh*-island violations with objects, as in (20) (*What$_i$ do you wonder how$_j$ to fix t_i t_j*).

The examples given so far have illustrated the behavior of θ-governed elements, subject only to Subjacency, with objects, and the behavior of non-θ-governed elements, subject to the antecedent government clause of the ECP, with adjuncts. Let us now turn to subjects. Since the subject position is not θ-marked by a head, it is not θ-governed; hence, extraction from this position is predicted to show *wh*-island effects. This prediction is apparently confirmed by ill-formed examples of the following type:

(56) *Who$_i$ do you wonder [what$_j$ t_i painted t_j]

On the other hand, there is one major respect in which subject extraction differs from both object and adjunct extraction: the former exhibits *that-t* effects, but the latter does not. The relevant examples are (57)–(58), where (57), with no overt complementizer adjacent to the subject extraction site, is well formed, but (58), which contains a *that-t* configuration, is not. No comparable violation arises with objects, as in (59), or with adjuncts, as in (60).

(57) Who$_i$ do you believe [t_i is a painter]

(58) *Who$_i$ do you believe [that t_i is a painter]

(59) Who$_i$ do you believe [(that) Peter likes t_i]

(60) How$_i$ do you believe [(that) Peter fixes it t_i]

The relevant configuration for *that-t* violations is provided in (61).

(61)

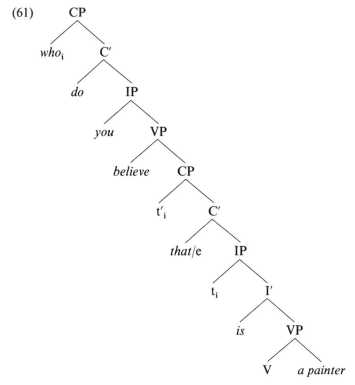

Here, under the theory outlined in (41)–(49), movement from t_i to the next landing site (the Spec of CP position t'_i) creates no violation, whether the embedded C is overt or not. In order to predict *that-t* violations as violations of antecedent government, the notion of minimality barrier must be introduced, as in (62). As before, the exceptional status of I is confirmed, since I′ cannot be a minimality barrier. Furthermore, unlike other barriers, minimality barriers do not count for both Subjacency and government, but only for government, as in (63).

(62) β is a minimality barrier for α iff β is an X′ (other than I′), β dominates α, and the head of β, X, is lexical (X other than α).

(63) Minimality barriers are barriers only for government.

With these notions in place, consider (61). If the embedded C is lexical, then C′ is a minimality barrier for t_i. This means that movement to the Spec of CP position t'_i is blocked by antecedent government, because one barrier is crossed. Suppose, however, that the embedded C is empty. Then C′ is not a minimality barrier for t_i, and t_i can move to the Spec of CP position t'_i without crossing any barriers, hence satisfying antecedent government. This explains the data in (57)–(58). As for (59), objects are predicted not to display *that-t* effects because they satisfy the ECP under the θ-government clause. The fact that I' is never a barrier means that (62)–(63) have no consequences for movement (of objects) across I' projections. However, a technical problem arises with respect to movement across V', which should always be a minimality barrier. This is solved by assuming that in the absence of a Spec of VP, V' is not projected and VP remains the only projection of V.

Finally, consider adjuncts. Essentially following Lasnik and Saito (1984), it is assumed that the relevant level for the satisfaction of antecedent government by traces in $\bar{\text{A}}$-position, and hence by adjuncts, is LF, as stated in (64), and that at LF *that* can systematically delete.

(64) Antecedent government applies to $\bar{\text{A}}$-traces at LF.

If so, then adjuncts are predicted not to display *that-t* effects, as the example in (60) indeed attests. Similarly, the theory predicts the contrast between (57)–(58) and (65).

(65) Who$_i$ do you believe [$_{CP}$ t'''_i (that) [$_{IP}$ I [$_{VP}$ t''_i said
     [$_{CP}$ t'_i [$_{IP}$ t_i is a painter]]]]]

In (57)–(58) the subject trace must be antecedent-governed at S-structure; as we have seen, it is so governed in the absence of *that*, as in (57), but not in the presence of *that*, as in (58). In (65), on the other hand, only intermediate traces are found on either side of *that*—namely, t''_i and t'''_i. Since intermediate traces are in $\bar{\text{A}}$-position, they only need to satisfy antecedent government at LF. Crucially, *that* can delete at LF, eliminating the minimality barrier it defines. Thus, (65) is well formed, whether *that* is present or absent at S-structure.

Head movement and A-movement remain to be accounted for. Head movement must satisfy antecedent government, since a head cannot be θ-governed. Antecedent government in turn correctly derives the descriptive generalization on head movement, the Head Movement Constraint. Consider for instance the contrast between (11) and (13), repeated here.

(11) Will$_i$ [Bill t_i [have finished his work]]

(13) *Have$_i$ [Bill will [t_i finished his work]]

Suppose that the base-generated position of the higher auxiliary in (11) and (13) corresponds to the I position in (41), and the position of the lower auxiliary to the V position in (41). Movement from the I to the C

position satisfies antecedent government, since neither I′ not IP is ever a
barrier except by inheritance. However, movement from the V to the C
position crosses at least two barriers, VP and IP, the latter in this case a
barrier by inheritance. Thus, (13) violates Subjacency as well as antecedent
government.

The antecedent government clause of the ECP also accounts for
A-movement. One problem that the theory faces, however, is that movement from the object position in (41) to the Spec of IP position is blocked
by the VP barrier. Of course, such movement must be allowed in order for
passive sentences to be generated, as in (66).

(66) John$_i$ was [hit t$_i$]

Since a movement dependency will in general relate the V and I positions
in (41), Chomsky (1986a) proposes that this dependency and the object-
to-subject dependency can be combined, allowing the latter to bypass the
VP barrier. A second problem is that the theory cannot predict that
A-movement is subject to antecedent government, since the trace of
A-movement typically is θ-governed. This fact must therefore be stipulated, as in (67).

(67) If α is an A-trace, α is antecedent-governed.

We are now in a position to draw some preliminary conclusions. Let us
consider first the empirical predictions of the theory, limiting ourselves to
two sets of data discussed by Chomsky (1986a). First, it is evident that the
theory faces empirical difficulties in the area of extractions across Ns.
Nothing in the theory predicts differences between objects of Ns and
objects of Vs. Thus, if complex NP islands like those in (32)–(33) are
characterized by a CP in the object position of N, the CP is predicted to
be L-marked, exactly like an object of V, and hence not to be a barrier. As
a result, such constructions are not expected to violate Subjacency. Second, the theory does not account for complex wh-island behaviors. In
particular, the interaction of wh-islands with Tense as in (35) can be
captured only by stipulation, essentially by assuming that a tensed IP is an
inherent barrier. Similarly, the ill-formedness of multiple wh-island violations, as in (37), must be attributed to an enrichment of the mechanism
that computes Subjacency violations, such that barriers crossed at different stages of the derivation can be cumulated. These and other problems
will be considered in detail in chapter 2. For the time being, all the island
behaviors predicted by the theory, either in a principled way or by stipulation, are summarized in table 1.1.

Table 1.1
Island predictions made by Chomsky's (1986a) theory

		θ-governed $\bar{\text{A}}$-trace	Non-θ-governed $\bar{\text{A}}$-trace/A-trace
Subjacency			
	Subject island	*	*
	Adjunct island	*	*
	Relative island	*	*
	Tense island	*	*
	Multiple *wh*-islands	*	*
ECP			
	Wh-island	OK	*
	That-t	OK	*

Considering next the conceptual framework that the theory offers for the locality problem, we find that it requires at least three stipulations. The first concerns the systematically exceptional behavior of the projections of I built into definitions (45) and (62) and condition (48). The second is that A-movement is always subject to antecedent government, though its traces are always θ-governed, as in (67); this must be added to the stipulation inherited from Lasnik and Saito (1984) that traces in $\bar{\text{A}}$-position are subject to antecedent government only at LF, as in (64). A third concerns the role of minimality barriers, which are stipulated to be relevant for government but not for Subjacency, as in (63).

However, notwithstanding these drawbacks, the theory has a conceptually important advantage. Within a barrier-based approach to locality it is at least in principle possible to think of all locality conditions on movement as being based on a single notion of locality domain, or barrier. Thus, although the disjunction between Subjacency and the ECP survives, as well as the disjunction between θ-government and antecedent government within the ECP, the theory appears to incorporate no principled obstacle to unification. This of course is crucial for our discussion.

1.3 Antecedent-Based Solutions

Antecedent-based solutions to the locality problem have also been proposed. This type of solution is represented by the Generalized Binding theory of Aoun (1985), which makes crucial use of a rigid notion of antecedent, or SUBJECT, and by Rizzi's (1990) Relativized Minimality, which makes crucial use of a relative notion of antecedent. Consider the latter first. Relativized Minimality is essentially a theory of the ECP component of locality. According to Rizzi (1990), the ECP reduces to a proper head government requirement, as in (68). Proper head government is government and c-command by a head, as in (69), where β c-commands α only if the first branching node that dominates β dominates α (Reinhart 1976). Adopting Chomsky's (1986a) terminology, β is then said to m-command α only if the first maximal projection that dominates β dominates α.

(68) *ECP*
A trace must be properly head-governed.

(69) X properly head-governs Y iff X head-governs and c-commands Y.

Both head government and antecedent government are crucially constrained by Relativized Minimality, as in (70).

(70) *Relativized Minimality*
X α-governs Y (α = head or antecedent) only if there is no Z such that
a. Z is a typical potential α-governor for Y, and
b. Z c-commands Y and does not c-command X.

The notion of typical potential α-governor that enters into (70), where α ranges over head and antecedent, is in turn defined as in (71) and (72) for head government and antecedent government, respectively.

(71) Z is a typical potential head governor for Y iff Z is a head m-commanding Y.

(72) Z is a typical potential antecedent governor for Y,

$$\text{Y in an} \begin{cases} \text{A-chain iff Z is an A-Spec} \\ \bar{\text{A}}\text{-chain iff Z is an } \bar{\text{A}}\text{-Spec} \\ \text{head chain iff Z is a head} \end{cases} \text{c-commanding Y.}$$

Antecedent government now becomes a requirement on chains. This is not to say, however, that antecedent government becomes a requirement on movement in general. The crucial assumption is that referential indices are licensed by the assignment of a referential θ-role, as in (73); all and only those elements that are assigned a referential index can then form a binding dependency, as in (74).

(73) A referential index must be licensed by a referential θ-role.

(74) X binds Y iff X c-commands Y, and X and Y have the same referential index.

Elements that are *not* assigned a referential index must indeed form a chain, where a chain is partially defined in terms of antecedent government, as in (75). Antecedent government itself is defined as in (76).

(75) $(\alpha_1, \ldots, \alpha_n)$ is a chain only if for all i, α_i antecedent-governs α_{i+1}.

(76) X antecedent-governs Y iff X and Y are nondistinct, X c-commands Y, and Relativized Minimality is satisfied.

Let us consider how this theory works. Consider first *wh*-island violations, which constitute the crucial test for the disjunction between θ-government and antecedent government. Relevant examples are again (20) and (21), repeated here.

(20)   What$_i$ do you wonder [how$_j$ to fix t_i t_j]

(21)   *How$_i$ do you wonder [what$_j$ to fix t_j t_i]

In Rizzi's (1990) terms, the object *wh*-phrase is assigned a referential θ-role in (20), which licenses a referential index under (73). Hence, the *wh*-phrase can form a dependency through binding, as in (74), which must satisfy head government, as in (68), but not antecedent government. Of course, head government is satisfied, the head governor being V, and (20) is predicted to be well formed. Now consider (21). The adjunct *wh*-phrase is not assigned a referential index under (73) because it is not assigned a referential θ-role. This means that it can only form a dependency if it forms a chain in the technical sense of the term, as in (75). This in turn means that it must satisfy antecedent government, as defined in (76). Now suppose that the adjunct in (21) is generated under the embedded IP, like t_i in (55). In the presence of a *wh*-phrase in the embedded Spec of CP, its next possible landing site is adjoined to the matrix VP, t'_i in (55). Movement from t_i to t'_i is blocked by Relativized Minimality precisely because a typical potential antecedent governor intervenes between t_i and t'_i in the form of the *wh*-phrase *what$_j$* in the Spec of CP. Hence, the ungrammaticality of (21) is again correctly predicted.

This theory predicts that subjects will pattern with objects rather than with adjuncts with respect to extraction, since they will typically be assigned a referential index. Indeed, it is possible to argue that *wh*-island effects with subjects differ substantially from *wh*-island effects with adjuncts. In particular, adjunct extraction out of a *wh*-island produces a violation at whichever point in the extraction path the *wh*-island is found. The violation in (21) is therefore parallel to the violation in (77), where the adjunct extraction site and the *wh*-island belong to two different sentences.

(77) *How$_i$ do you wonder [whether to believe [he is fixing it t$_i$]]

However, if the *wh*-island is not immediately adjacent to the subject extraction site, no (strong) violation ensues, as in (56), repeated here, versus (78).

(56) *Who$_i$ do you wonder [what$_j$ t$_i$ painted t$_j$]

(78) Who$_i$ do you wonder [whether to believe [t$_i$ is painting it]]

All theories under consideration correctly predict the behavior of the adjunct in (77). Differences arise, however, with respect to (56) and (78). Chomsky's (1986a) account of (56) in terms of antecedent government predicts that (78) is as unacceptable as (77). Given that the subject being extracted has a referential index and is not subject to antecedent government, Rizzi's (1990) theory predicts the well-formedness of (78), leaving the ungrammaticality of (56) to be accounted for. If adjacency to the subject extraction site is in fact crucial to *wh*-island violations with subjects, then these are essentially similar to *that-t* violations, as in (57)–(58), repeated here.

(57) Who$_i$ do you believe [t$_i$ is a painter]

(58) *Who$_i$ do you believe [that t$_i$ is a painter]

Rizzi (1990) indeed proposes a unified solution to *that-t* and *wh-t* violations. Remember that traces must be properly head-governed under (68). But consider the configuration in (61). The embedded I, *is*, that head-governs the subject, t_i, does not c-command it in Reinhart's (1976) sense, and hence does not properly head-govern it under (68). However, in order for this trace to be properly head-governed, it is sufficient that the embedded I and C agree, so that the subject is properly head-governed from the C position. Indeed, Rizzi (1990) takes the apparent absence of an embedded C in the well-formed (57) to be just a reflex of I-C agreement; quite simply, he assumes the zero form of C to be the agreeing form in English. The ill-formedness of (58) is then also explained, on the assumption *that* that is a nonagreeing form of C. *Wh-t* violations can also be viewed as a reflex of I-C agreement, since if I and C agree, the Spec of CP and the Spec of IP must also agree, and the Spec of CP cannot be filled by a *wh*-phrase that disagrees with the subject in the Spec of IP.

These subject extraction phenomena constitute one of three empirical areas where Rizzi's (1990) theory makes new predictions. The second involves the Relativized Minimality constraint in (70) itself. We have seen how this constraint accounts for *wh*-island violations with adjuncts. According to Rizzi, there are at least two other types of *wh*-islands: inner islands, created by a negation (Ross 1984), and pseudo-opacity islands, created by a floating quantifier (Obenauer 1976, 1984). Inner islands produce a violation with adjuncts, as in (79), but not with arguments, as in (80); for pseudo-opacity islands also produce a violation with adjuncts, as exemplified by the French construction in (81).

(79) What$_i$ didn't he repair t$_i$

(80) *How$_i$ didn't he repair it t$_i$

(81) *Comment$_i$ a-t-il beaucoup$_j$ acheté [t$_j$ de bouquins] t$_i$
     how did he   a lot   buy   of books

Relativized Minimality easily accounts for both inner and pseudo-opacity islands, given the assumption that the elements that create them (the negative *not* and floating quantifiers) occupy an $\bar{\text{A}}$-Spec position, possibly Spec of VP. Now consider the structures in (82)–(83), corresponding respectively to (79) and (81). If we assume that the adjunct in (79) and (81) is generated under VP, its movement from a VP-internal position to the Spec of CP is blocked under (76) by a potential antecedent— namely, the negation or floating quantifier in the Spec of VP. Thus, Rizzi's Relativized Minimality theory is able to account for (79) and (81); Chomsky's barriers theory is not.

(82)

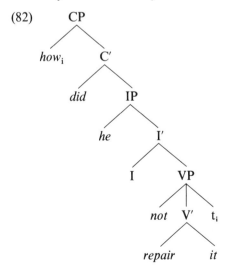

(83)

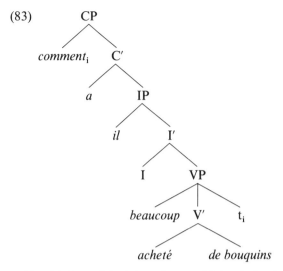

The third empirical domain on which Rizzi (1990) concentrates is related to the referential/nonreferential distinction that he draws, which replaces the θ-governed/non-θ-governed distinction proposed by Chomsky (1986a). Rizzi adduces three arguments to support his distinction. First, he argues that adverbs that obligatorily cooccur with certain Vs are θ-marked by them, and hence θ-governed; however, under extraction they behave exactly like adjuncts, causing wh-islands violations, as in (84). He suggests that the same is true of idiom chunk NPs, as in (85), and of measure phrases, as in (86).

(84) *[How well]$_i$ do you wonder [whether he worded his letter t$_i$]

(85) *[What headway]$_i$ do you wonder [whether he has made t$_i$]

(86) *[How many kilos]$_i$ do you wonder [whether he weighs t$_i$]

The shift from the notion of θ-government to the notion of referential index allows the ungrammaticality of (84)–(86) to be correctly predicted. Indeed, none of the wh-phrases involved has a referential index, since though each of them is θ-marked, it can be assumed not to be referentially θ-marked, as required by the licensing condition on referential indices in (73). This aspect of the theory is explored in more detail by Cinque (1991), who proposes that it should be extended to the contrast between (87) and (88), where an existential and a universal quantifier, respectively, are extracted from a wh-island, and to the contrast between (89) and (90), where a D(iscourse)-linked and a non-D-linked wh-phrase, respectively, in the sense of Pesetsky (1987), are extracted from a wh-island. Cinque proposes that these contrasts can be accounted for, if existential quantifiers and D-linked wh-phrases have a referential index, whereas universal quantifiers and non-D-linked wh-phrases do not.

(87)   [Some museums]$_i$ I wonder [whether to visit t$_i$]

(88)   *[Every museum]$_i$ I wonder [whether to visit t$_i$]

(89)   [Which car]$_i$ did you wonder [how$_j$ to repair t$_i$ t$_j$]

(90)   *[What the hell]$_i$ did you wonder [how$_j$ to repair t$_i$ t$_j$]

Rizzi's theory also predicts that head dependencies are subject to antecedent government, on the assumption that heads are not associated with referential indices. As for A-dependencies, it appears to be impossible to deny them referential indices, since A-movement typically involves referential phrases. However, Rizzi observes that the θ-Criterion of Chomsky (1981) applies to chains. If so, then because A-dependencies must satisfy the θ-Criterion, they must also conform to the chain format, independently of whether or not referential indices are involved, and they therefore must satisfy antecedent government.

Before we attempt to evaluate Rizzi's theory, let us consider the second antecedent-based solution to the locality problem, proposed by Aoun (1985). Aoun argues that the ECP can be eliminated in favor of binding theory. Thus, Chomsky's (1981) binding conditions, concerned entirely with A-binding, are extended to X-binding, as in (91), where X-binding ranges over both A- and Ā-binding. The definition of governing category relevant for (91) is essentially preserved from Chomsky (1981), as in (92). However, the definition of accessible SUBJECT is generalized as in (93), so that accessibility fails when coindexing violates any grammatical principle, not just Chomsky's (1981) i-within-i Condition.

(91)   *Generalized Binding Conditions*
       A. An anaphor must be X-bound in its governing category.
       B. A pronominal must be X-free in its governing category.
       C. A name must be A-free.

(92)   β is a governing category for α iff β is the minimal category containing α, a governor for α, and a SUBJECT accessible to α.

(93)   β is accessible to α iff β c-commands α and coindexing of α and β does not violate any grammatical principles.

Consider then an object Ā-trace, as in the wh-island configuration in (20). As a variable, t_i in (20) must be A-free under Generalized Binding

Condition C in (91). On the other hand, since all traces are assumed to be anaphoric, Generalized Binding Condition A in (91) also applies to t_i in (20), requiring it to be X-bound in its governing category. But according to (92), what is the governing category of t_i? No subject can be an accessible SUBJECT for t_i under (93), since coindexing between it and a subject would make it A-bound and hence lead to a violation of Generalized Binding Condition C. Furthermore, no Agr can be an accessible SUBJECT for t_i, since every Agr is coindexed with a subject, and coindexing between t_i and a subject is excluded as before. However, it is assumed that in the absence of any governing category, as defined in (92), the root sentence counts as a governing category for an anaphor, as in (94).

(94) A root sentence is a governing category for an anaphor.

If so, then Generalized Binding for an object $\bar{A}$-trace, such as t_i in (20), reduces to the requirement that the trace must be bound within the root sentence. This correctly predicts that, as in (20), $\bar{A}$-movement can take place in one step, bypassing any *wh*-islands on the way.

Next consider subject $\bar{A}$-traces, such as t_i in (56). Crucially, Aoun (1985) assumes an S/S' structure of the traditional type. For his results to be replicated within current theories of X-bar structure, it is necessary to assume (much the same way as Chomsky (1986a)) that IP is defective, so that β in the definition of governing category in (92) is other than IP. Again, under (91) t_i in (56) must be bound in its governing category. Furthermore, under (93) the Agr with which t_i is coindexed counts as an accessible SUBJECT for it. Hence, under (92) the governing category for t_i is the embedded CP, IP being defective by stipulation. Within CP t_i can be $\bar{A}$-bound from the Spec of CP position. But if t_i is not bound from this position, a violation of Generalized Binding Condition A ensues. Thus, Generalized Binding Condition A predicts the antecedent government effects for subjects that are indeed found in (56).

Finally, consider adjunct $\bar{A}$-traces, such as the one in the *wh*-island configuration in (21). The crucial aspect of Aoun's theory in this respect is that t_i in (21) does not count as a variable, because it is not referential. Thus, t_i is subject only to Generalized Binding Condition A. This in turn means that even if IP is defective, the embedded CP is a governing category for t_i under (92), since coindexing of the embedded subject or Agr with it does not produce any violation under (93). The antecedent government properties of adjunct $\bar{A}$-traces, specifically their inability to bypass *wh*-islands, are then correctly predicted by Generalized Binding Condition A. Of course, this condition also derives the antecedent government properties of A-movement and of A-binding of lexical anaphors and pronouns. Similarly, the antecedent government properties of head movement can be derived if, following Koopman (1984), head-to-head movement is viewed as an instance of A- rather than $\bar{\text{A}}$-movement.

One empirical domain with respect to which Aoun's (1985) theory differs from both Rizzi's (1990) and Chomsky's (1986a) is extraction from NPs. Remember that it is possible to extract an argument across a single nominal boundary, as in (32), but it is never possible to extract an adjunct across it, as in (34).

(32)   Who$_i$ did you see [many portraits of t$_i$]

(34)   *[With what kind of sleeves]$_i$ did you see [many sweaters t$_i$]

First consider (34). On the assumption that whatever fills the Spec of NP position, including Det as in (34), counts as the SUBJECT of NP, understood as the most prominent element in the phrase, the ungrammaticality of adjunct extraction from NP is immediately accounted for. NP indeed counts as a governing category for the adjunct in that it contains a SUBJECT accessible to it, and the crossing of NP violates Generalized Binding Condition A.

Next consider (32). The argument that undergoes extraction can be interpreted as either the subject or the object of N. If it is interpreted as the subject of N, then NP is not a governing category for it, on the assumption that there is no other accessible SUBJECT in NP. If on the other hand it is interpreted as the object of N, it can still move to the SUBJECT position first, so that its ability to be extracted follows as before. Such a theory predicts that if the SUBJECT position of an NP is independently filled, the object cannot be extracted. Crucially, Aoun (1985) claims that examples like (95) support this prediction:

(95)   *Who$_i$ did you see [my many portraits of t$_i$]

We are now in a position to draw conclusions from the discussion so far. It seems clear that Rizzi's (1990) theory inherits two important conceptions from Aoun's (1985). The first is the distinction between referential and nonreferential elements, which in both theories distinguishes adjuncts from objects. The second, and the reason why the two theories are grouped together here, is that in both cases antecedent government is based on a notion of accessible, or potential, antecedent. The main difference between the two theories is that Aoun (1985) proposes a rigid notion of antecedent, coinciding with the notion of SUBJECT, whereas Rizzi (1990) relativizes the notion of antecedent to the various types of dependencies.

From an empirical point of view, Aoun's (1985) theory has an advantage with respect to extraction from NPs, but not with respect to any of our other residual problems, such as the interaction of *wh*-islands with Tense. Rizzi's (1990) theory appears to have empirical advantages with respect to inner and pseudo-opacity islands, but has essentially the same problems as Chomsky's (1986a) theory with respect to extraction from NPs, interaction of *wh*-islands with Tense, and so on. In addition, there are islands, which Rizzi (1990) does not consider, that display the typical pattern of *wh*-, inner, and pseudo-opacity islands, in that adjuncts are sensitive to them but arguments are not. In the terminology of Cinque (1991), they include factive islands, created by verbs such as *regret* in (96), and extraposition islands, as in (97).

(96) *How$_i$ do you regret [that I behaved t$_i$]

(97) *How$_i$ is it a shame [that they behaved t$_i$]

Not being antecedent-based, these islands are problematic for Relativized Minimality, as much as for any theory considered so far.

The empirical predictions of Rizzi's (1990) theory are summarized in table 1.2. What is crucial for present purposes is the general conceptual structure of Rizzi's (1990) and Aoun's (1985) theories. In both cases, at least one non-antecedent-based condition (Subjacency) is required in addition to the proposed antecedent-based conditions. Hence, antecedent-

Table 1.2
Island predictions made by Rizzi's (1990) theory

		Indexed traces	Nonindexed traces/chains
Subjacency			
	Subject island	*	*
	Adjunct island	*	*
	Relative island	*	*
Antecedent government			
	Wh-island	OK	*
	Inner island	OK	*
	Pseudo-opacity island	OK	*
Head government			
	That-t	OK (object)/ * (subject)	OK

based theories appear to be fundamentally disjunctive and thus immediately excluded as candidates for a unified theory of locality.

1.4 Connectedness Solutions

Next we will take up connectedness solutions to the locality problem. These are solutions, such as the Connectedness Condition of Kayne (1983) and the Path Containment Condition of Pesetsky (1982), which are based entirely on the geometry of trees. In a sense, they are the opposite of antecedent-based solutions. First consider Kayne's (1983) proposal. Its crucial construct is the notion of g-projection, defined as in (98). In practice, a governor on the right, rather than on the left, always blocks the formation of g-projections in a language like English where canonical government, in the sense of (99), is left to right.

(98) Y is a g-projection of X iff
   a. Y is a projection of X or of a g-projection of X; or
   b. Y immediately dominates W and Z, where Z is a g-projection of X, and W and Z are in a canonical government configuration.

(99) W and Z are in a canonical government configuration iff V governs NP to its right in the language and W precedes Z; or V governs NP to its left in the language and Z precedes W.

Given the notion of g-projection in (98), a g-projection set of a category α is defined as the set of all g-projections of β, where β is a (head) governor for α, together with α itself, and any node that dominates α and does not dominate β, as in (100). The Connectedness Condition is formulated in terms of g-projection sets as in (101). Roughly speaking, given a set of empty categories $\alpha_1, \ldots, \alpha_n$ with antecedent β in a tree T, under (101) β together with the g-projection sets of $\alpha_1, \ldots, \alpha_n$ must constitute a subtree of T.

(100) G_α is the g-projection set of a category α, where β governs α, iff
   a. all g-projections of β belong to G_α
   b. α belongs to G_α and
   b'. if δ dominates α and does not dominate β, δ belongs to G_α.

(101) *Connectedness Condition*
   Let $\alpha_1, \ldots, \alpha_n$ be a maximal set of empty categories in a tree T such that for some β, all α_i are bound by β. Then β together with the g-projection sets of all α_i must constitute a subtree of T.

First, consider a trace in the object position of a V, as in the *wh*-island configuration in (20), repeated here.

(20) What$_i$ do you wonder [how$_j$ to fix t$_i$ t$_j$]

(101) requires that the antecedent for t_i (namely, the *wh*-phrase) be contained in a g-projection of the (head) governor for t_i (namely, V). In turn, g-projections as defined in (98)–(99) are sensitive only to the geometry of the tree and are not in any way sensitive to antecedent configurations. Thus, object extraction is indeed predicted not to be sensitive to the typical antecedent-based constraint (namely, *wh*-islands), as in (20).

Second, consider an object being extracted out of a subject island, as in (17), repeated here, whose configuration was illustrated earlier in (50).

(17) *What$_i$ does [explaining t$_i$] bother you

Since the object t_i is governed by V, the crucial question is whether there is a g-projection of V that contains the antecedent for it, namely, the *wh*-phrase. The embedded VP is a g-projection of V; the embedded IP is a g-projection of VP because I canonically governs VP; and the embedded CP is a g-projection of IP because C canonically governs IP. Thus, the embedded CP in (50) is a g-projection of V. However, the embedded CP in (50), being in subject position, is governed by the matrix I, but not canonically governed by it. This means that the matrix IP is not a g-projection of the embedded V; hence, the antecedent of t_i, the *wh*-phrase in the matrix Spec of CP, is not contained within a g-projection of its governor V. If so, Connectedness is violated; in other words, Connectedness correctly accounts for subject islands like the one in (17).

Third, consider an object being extracted out of an adjunct island, as in (18), repeated here, whose configuration was shown earlier in (51).

(18) *What$_i$ was Mary bothered [because Peter explained t$_i$]

Kayne's (1983) theory differs from all the ones considered so far in predicting such an extraction to be well formed. Indeed, the embedded CP in (51) is a g-projection of the V that governs t_i, very much like the embedded CP in (50). Unlike the subject CP in (50), however, the adjunct CP in (51) is in a canonical government configuration with its sister V'. Hence, the g-projection of the embedded V can be extended to the matrix VP in (51) and from there to the matrix CP, which includes the antecedent for t_i, namely, the *wh*-phrase. Examples like (18) are thus predicted to be well formed. Such a prediction is only apparently incorrect. Remember our discussion of the interaction of Tense with *wh*-islands, as in (35). If Tense indeed creates island effects, the presence of Tense in the adjunct in (18) is in itself sufficient to define a violation. We then expect extraction from an adjunct to be well formed if the adjunct is untensed. The prediction is arguably correct, given the relative well-formedness of examples like (102).

(102) What$_i$ did Peter leave [after explaining t$_i$]

Indeed, the contrast between (18) and (102) strengthens the Tense island problem for all theories under consideration, Kayne's (1983) included; moreover, (102) supports Connectedness over Chomsky's (1986a) Subjacency.

From the point of view of attempting to unify locality conditions, Connectedness obviously presents a fundamental problem. Let us again consider an object of V. When this object enters into an A-dependency, Connectedness may be a necessary condition on it, but it is certainly not a sufficient one, since the dependency must be strictly local even in the presence of an unbounded g-projection. A completely separate theory, not based uniquely on tree geometry, will then have to be invoked. Thus, Connectedness appears to be no more useful as a basis for a unified theory of locality than antecedent-based accounts, though for exactly opposite reasons.

Of course, saying that a principle based purely on tree geometry is not sufficient to encompass the whole of locality is not the same as showing that such a principle is unnecessary. In particular, apart from apparent exceptions to adjunct island violations like (102), independent evidence for Connectedness comes from parasitic gaps in the sense of Taraldsen 1981, Chomsky 1982, and much related work. In the parasitic gap phenomenon a single operator appears to bind two different variables. Kayne (1983) argues that Connectedness correctly predicts the contrast between (relatively) well-formed examples like (103)–(104) and ill-formed examples like (105).

(103)   A person who$_i$ [close friends of t$_i$] admire t_i

(104)   A person who$_i$ you admire t$_i$ [because you know [close friends of t$_i$]]

(105)   *A person who$_i$ you admire t$_i$ [because [close friends of t$_i$] become famous]

The relevant structures for (103)–(104) are (106)–(107), where the nodes marked 1 belong to the g-projection set of t_1 and the nodes marked 2 belong to the g-projection set of t_2.

(106)

(107)

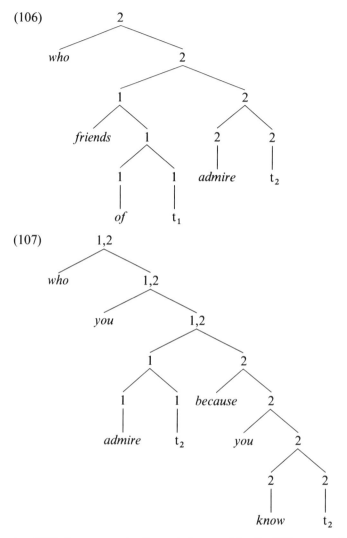

In (106) the t_1 g-projection set does not by itself form a subtree with the *wh*-phrase antecedent; but the t_2 g-projection set allows it to do so. Thus, descriptively, the potential subject island violation by t_1 is rescued by t_2. Notice that the g-projection set of t_2 is able to bypass the adjunct island in (107) without any assistance from the g-projection set of t_1. Indeed, we have seen that Connectedness, though predicting subject islands, does not predict adjunct islands.

By contrast with (106), consider (108), the relevant structure for (105).

(108)

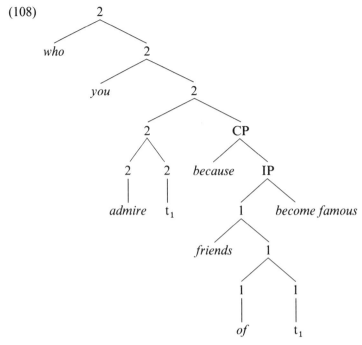

In (108) the g-projection set of t_1 stops at the subject node, as in (106), but contrary to (106), it forms a subtree distinct from the subtree formed by the g-projection set of t_2. Thus, in (108), contrary to (106), t_2 cannot rescue t_1 from its subject island violation.

Recall that under Chomsky's (1986a) Subjacency, relative clause islands are essentially a kind of adjunct islands, since relative clauses are attached in adjunct-like position within NP, as in (52). By contrast, Kayne's (1983) theory predicts that relative clauses (just like adjuncts) will not give rise to Connectedness violations, since they enter canonical government configurations (i.e., they are attached to the right in English). Thus, the parallelism with adjuncts is maintained, but the predictions are reversed. Examples like (109), with the structure in (110), indeed appear to support Connectedness. The g-projection set of t_1 bypasses the relative clause (island) in (110) without assistance from the g-projection set of t_2; the latter is then instrumental in rescuing the potential subject island violation.

(109) A person who$_i$ [people that talk to t$_i$] usually end up fascinated
       with t$_i$

(110)

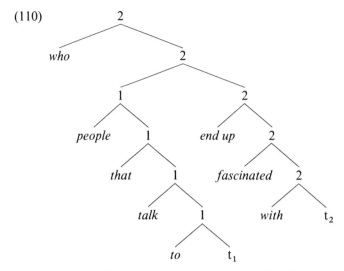

Although relative clause island violations like (19), repeated here, are clearly ungrammatical, this can be attributed to the same Tense effect that causes the ungrammaticality of adjunct island violations like (18). If so, extraction from untensed relative clauses is expected to be grammatical, as in (111) and (112), where Italian differs from English in allowing overt *wh*-phrases in infinitival relatives.

(18)   *What$_i$ was Mary bothered [because Peter explained t$_i$]

(19)   *What$_i$ do you know [the girl [that explained t$_i$]

(111)   *The student that $_i$ I know [a book [O$_j$ to give t$_j$ to t$_i$]]

(112)   *Il libro   che$_i$ conosco [uno studente [a cui$_j$ dare   t$_i$ t$_j$]]
         the book that I know   a student   to whom to give

The fact that (111)–(112) are *not* grammatical can be attributed to a complex NP island effect. Indeed, (111)–(112) appear to have the same status as examples like (33), with extraction from a CP object of N. Connectedness then brings to the fore the problem of complex NP islands, as well as the problem of Tense islands in (18) versus (102).

The predictions that Connectedness makes for simple (nonparasitic) extractions are summarized in table 1.3. The table mentions argument traces only, because Kayne (1983) does not discuss the extraction of adjuncts. Thus, this theory leaves open the question of any differences between the behavior of adjuncts and the behavior of arguments.

A theory conceptually close to Kayne's (1983) is Pesetsky's (1982), which is based on a notion related to g-projection, namely, the notion

Table 1.3
Island predictions made by Kayne's (1983) theory

		Argument traces
Connectedness		
	Subject island	*
	Adjunct island	OK

"path." A path is technically defined in (113) as the set of all nodes that dominate a trace up to the first maximal projection that also dominates its antecedent.

(113) If t is locally $\bar{A}$-bound by α, β is the first nonlexical node dominating t, and β' is the first maximal projection dominating α, then the path between t and α is the set of nodes P including β, β' and all and only γ such that γ dominates β and γ does not dominate β'.

The major condition on paths is the Path Containment Condition (115), stated in terms of overlapping paths (114). In effect, (115) allows nested dependencies and disallows crossing ones.

(114) Two paths overlap iff their intersection is nonnull and nonsingleton.

(115) *Path Containment Condition (PCC)*
      If two paths overlap, one must contain the other.

Consider the standard contrast between adjunct extraction and object extraction from *wh*-islands, as in the familiar examples (20) and (21), repeated here along with the relevant structure (116).

(20)   What$_i$ do you wonder [how$_j$ to fix t$_i$ t$_j$]

(21)   *How$_i$ do you wonder [what$_j$ to fix t$_j$ t$_i$]

(116)

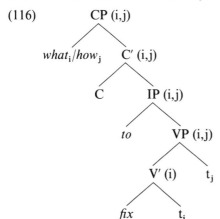

Pesetsky's (1982) theory treats this contrast as a PCC effect. In (116) the path created by object extraction includes the embedded V′, VP, and so on, as indicated; even assuming that the adjunct is attached as a sister to V, the path created by adjunct extraction includes the embedded VP and so on, but not V′. The two extraction paths will of course overlap, since they have common members such as VP. Suppose then that the object moves to a higher position than the adjunct, as in (20). If so, the path of the object completely contains the path of the adjunct, since it extends farther downward with respect to V′, as well as farther upward by hypothesis. Thus, the PCC is not violated. But suppose that the adjunct moves higher than the object, as in (21). Then by hypothesis the path of the adjunct extends farther upward than the path of the object; but the former, which does not include V′, cannot completely contain the latter, which does. Thus, the PCC is violated.

Next consider subject island violations, as in (17).

(17) *What$_i$ does [explaining t$_i$] bother you

Prima facie, the PCC does not make any predictions concerning such violations since a single dependency is involved, rather than two interacting dependencies. However, Pesetsky (1982) postulates that a dependency is systematically established between the I and C positions of any given sentence. This means that the relevant structure for a subject island violation is as in (117).

(117)

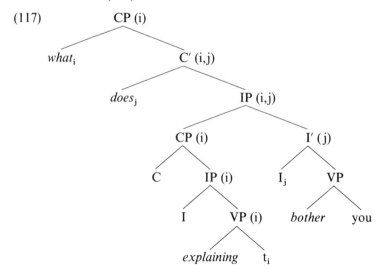

The path between the matrix I and C, which are involved in overt head-to-head movement in (117), contains I', IP, and C'. The path for the extraction from the subject island never includes I', but it does include a number of nodes, such as the embedded CP, which are not included in the I-to-C path. Thus, extraction from a subject inevitably violates the PCC.

It is evident that the PCC has the same basic problem as Connectedness with respect to unifying locality theory. Both of these accounts attempt to make use only of the pure geometry of trees. From the unification point of view, this approach has the fundamental fault that it must be supplemented by some nongeometrical approach, presumably an antecedent-based one, to account for typical antecedent government dependencies such as A-movement. On the other hand, to the extent that the PCC, unlike Connectedness, takes the interaction of different paths into account, it appears to be redundant with any antecedent-based constraint. If so, the PCC can be argued to have an additional conceptual disadvantage with respect to Connectedness.

Of course, showing that the PCC is insufficient is entirely different from showing that it is unnecessary. There is a particular series of contrasts, which look prima facie like crossing versus nesting contrasts, that the PCC accounts for, but other locality conditions do not. Thus, if a head has both an object and a prepositional object, it appears that the prepositional object can be extracted across the object, but not vice versa, as in (118)–(119).

(118)   [Which violins]$_i$ are these sonatas easy [O$_j$ [to play t$_j$ on t$_i$]]

(119)   *[Which sonatas]$_i$ are these violins easy [O$_j$ [to play t$_i$ on t$_j$]]

In terms of the PCC, the prepositional object path contains at least one node, PP, which the direct object path does not contain. Thus, if the prepositional object is extracted farther than the direct object, as in (118), the path of the former contains that of the latter, as required by the PCC. On the other hand, if the direct object is extracted farther, as in (119), its path cannot contain that of the prepositional object (and vice versa), and the PCC is violated. Contrasts such as these thus constitute crucial empirical arguments in favor of the PCC.

1.5   The Locality Solution

With the previous sections as background, I would now like to present my own solution to the locality problem, as an informal introduction to the discussion to follow. The fundamental ideas behind this solution are extremely simple and require no special technical apparatus. I assume that every lexical item and every other element individuated by lexical features of any sort is assigned what I call a *categorial index*. Roughly, categorial indices are indices of content. In the case of NPs these indices can be identified with the referential indices commonly used to express both anaphoric and movement dependencies. Thus, I am not so much introducing a new primitive, as extending an already existing one. Notice that to the extent that so-called referential indices are standardly used to express movement dependencies involving Vs rather than NPs, they are no longer referential in any identifiable sense of the term. Rizzi (1990) makes the same argument but reaches the opposite conclusion: namely, that referential indices should be maintained as such, and restricted to elements that indeed have referential content.

There is also a second type of index in the grammar, which I call an *address*, borrowing the term and in part the conception from Vergnaud (1985). Roughly speaking, addresses are indices of position and differ from categorial indices in being relational. Thus, in general a position Case-marked by a head is addressed by the head; in particular, we can assume that the address assigned to the Case-marked position corresponds to the categorial index of the Case-marking head. Again, then, addresses do not so much introduce a new primitive in the grammar, as encode an already existing relation, Case assignment by a head.

Each of the five dependencies considered earlier (anaphora as in (1)–(4), A-movement as in (5)–(8), head movement as in (9)–(13), Ā-movement of arguments as in (14)–(19), and Ā-movement of adjuncts as in (24)–(26)) can be established on the basis of a categorial index. An antecedent for a trace, anaphor, or pronoun can be defined simply as an element that shares a categorial index with it. Furthermore, each of the five dependencies is ordered by c-command. Thus, the antecedent, with which the categorial index resides, c-commands the dependent element, with which it shares the index.

Crucially, the five dependencies differ with respect to addresses. Three of them in fact involve a trace without an address. From θ-theory and Case theory, it follows that neither an A-trace nor the trace of a V or I head (or its maximal projection) is ever Case-marked; hence, such traces are never addressed. Whether an adjunct Ā-trace is Case-marked or not, we can assume that it is never Case-marked by a head; hence, it is never addressed either.

By contrast, Ā-traces of arguments typically are addressed, by V if they are assigned accusative Case, and by I if they are assigned nominative

Case. The same is true of lexical anaphors and pronouns. However, the notion of address serves to distinguish argument $\bar{\text{A}}$-traces from lexical anaphors and pronouns. The antecedent of an anaphor or pronoun will be independently Case-marked and hence addressed differently from the referentially dependent element. The antecedent of an argument $\bar{\text{A}}$-trace, typically a *wh*-phrase, will not be independently Case-marked and hence will not be independently addressed either.

Since dependencies can be defined on the basis of categorial indices and since an address is just another type of index, dependencies ought to be definable on the basis of a shared address as well. Let us consider the five dependencies in turn, each of which is well defined as a categorial index dependency. An (antecedent, anaphor) or (antecedent, pronoun) pair cannot in general form an address-based dependency for the simple reason that the two members of the dependency have different addresses; it would be like trying to form a categorial index dependency between two names. In the case of head movement and $\bar{\text{A}}$-movement of adjuncts, movement is from a nonaddressed position to another nonaddressed position. No address-based dependency can be formed because these positions have no address to share. Finally, consider the dependencies corresponding to A-movement and to $\bar{\text{A}}$-movement of arguments. In the former the trace is not addressed, but the antecedent generally is. In the latter the trace is generally addressed, but the antecedent is not. Thus, in the case of an A-chain the address of the antecedent can in principle be transmitted downward to the trace, whereas in the case of an argument $\bar{\text{A}}$-chain the address can be transmitted upward from the trace to the antecedent. Only in $\bar{\text{A}}$-chains is the direction of transmission congruent with the general direction of transmission of features and/or indices under movement; thus, we can assume that argument $\bar{\text{A}}$-chains are well formed both as address-based dependencies and as categorial index dependencies, and that A-chains are not.

To sum up: $\bar{\text{A}}$-dependencies involving arguments are distinguished from all other dependencies, in that they are well formed not only as categorial index dependencies but also as address-based ones. This means that one component of the unification problem for locality theory is solved. Dependencies with strict locality effects differ from other dependencies only in that the latter but not the former are well formed as address-based dependencies.

The formal notions involved are extremely simple. Categorial indices can be associated simply with lexicality, as in (119). Addressing can be defined as Case marking by a head, as in (120), and, adopting the cover term *sequence* for both categorial index and address-based dependencies, a sequence can be defined simply as in (121).

(119) α has a categorial index if α is lexical.

(120) α has an address if there is a head β that Case-marks α.

(121) $(\alpha_1, \ldots, \alpha_n)$ is a sequence iff for all i, α_i is coindexed with and c-commands α_{i+1}.

It should be stressed again that (119)–(121) represent more a reorganization of the existing theory of grammar than an enrichment of it. In particular, (121) needs to be stated anyway in order to define a chain. In the proposed theory, of course, a chain will be defined simply as a sequence, which also satisfies certain other requirements.

We are now in a position to approach the second part of the unification problem. Given that the crucial difference between strictly local dependencies and all others is that only the latter can be construed as address-based dependencies, do their different locality behaviors follow from this single difference, without any disjunction being stipulated between them in the locality theory itself?

I assume that the locality theory for categorial index sequences reduces to a condition like (122)—that is, essentially the antecedent government clause of the ECP and/or binding theory formulated as a biconditional. In (122) *dependent element* is a cover term for traces and anaphors, the only nondependent elements relevant in this context being pronouns. A sequence is said to satisfy government iff all links of the sequence satisfy it. Government in turn is defined, as in Chomsky 1986a, as holding between two positions just in case no barrier is crossed.

(122) *Locality*
        α is a dependent element iff there is an antecedent β for α and a sequence $(\beta, \ldots, \alpha)$ that satisfies government.

In order to prove that (122) represents the locality theory for categorial index sequences, we need to prove that (122) derives Subjacency as well. This is indeed the case, as I will argue in chapter 2, given the appropriate definition of barrier. Right now, however, the crucial issue is to determine the locality theory for address-based sequences. If it is also found to be (122), then the unification problem is essentially solved.

Consider for instance the structure in (123), which is a shortened bisentential structure with an embedded *wh*-island, where each structure contains a lexical V head and a functional C head.

(123)

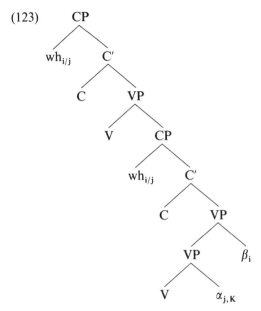

IP projections are omitted here only in order to avoid technical discussions that are properly left for chapter 2. The embedded clause contains a direct object, α, and an adjunct, where again for simplicity the adjunct is adjoined to VP. Crucially, the adjunct is associated only with a categorial index, but the object is associated with both a categorial index and an address (notated with a capital subscript). The question is whether the single locality principle in (122) correctly predicts that the adjunct cannot move across the *wh*-island, as in (21), but the argument can, as in (20).

First consider the adjunct. This can move only if a well-formed categorial index dependency can be created. Since β_i in (123) is adjoined to VP, the first barrier for it is the embedded CP. But suppose that its next possible landing site, the Spec of CP, is already filled by wh_j. If so, β_i can only move by crossing the CP barrier, and Locality is correctly predicted to be violated, as in (21). This prediction is of course more or less shared by all current theories.

Next consider the direct object. α_j can move if it can enter into either a well-formed categorial index dependency or a well-formed address-based dependency. α_j cannot ultimately enter into a well-formed categorial index dependency for the same reason that β_i cannot, given the presence of another *wh*-phrase in the Spec of the embedded CP. However, consider the address-based alternative. None of the positions in (123) is addressed, except for α_j itself. Under the simplest conception of coaddressing, α_j can then form an address-based sequence with any of the positions in (123), yielding for instance the sequence (wh, C, V, C, V, α) of address K. If so, α_j is correctly predicted to satisfy government, as in (20).

To sum up once again: $\bar{A}$-traces of arguments differ from $\bar{A}$-traces of adjuncts, anaphors, pronouns, A-traces, and head traces, in that they can form address-based dependencies as well as categorial index dependencies. The two types of dependencies are subject to the same locality principle, (122). The different locality effects they give rise to follow without stipulation from their own different properties. This result has been shown to hold for the configuration in (123). But if (122) is correct, it can also be shown to hold for any other configuration. If so, then it is not the case that there are different locality theories for different types of dependencies; rather, there is only one locality theory, (122).

In sketching the proposed theory, I have claimed that it is superior because it eliminates a set of disjunctions—in other words, because it is simpler and/or because the grammar that includes it is more highly modular in nature. But can it also be distinguished from other current theories in terms of its empirical predictions? The answer to such a question is always fraught with difficulties, since most predictions require decisions quite independent of the theories being evaluated. However, three points can be made in this regard. First, most current theories of extraction face difficulties concerning complex NP island violations with sentences in the object position of N, as in (33), repeated here. This is a problem common to all theories of Subjacency based on the CED, including Chomsky's (1986a).

(33) *Who$_i$ did you see [many attempts [to portray t$_i$]]

Second, with the exception of Aoun's (1985) theory, they do not make clear predictions with respect to extractions from simple NPs, specifically with respect to the impossibility of extracting adjuncts, as in (34); nor do they make clear predictions with respect to the impossibility of extracting from definites, as in (36).

(34) *[With what kind of sleeves]$_i$ did you see [many sweaters t$_i$]

(36) *Who$_i$ did you see [the many portraits of t$_i$]

Third, there is no nonstipulative approach to Tense effects and to their interaction with *wh*-islands, as in (35), or to the contrast between double and triple *wh*-extractions, as in (37).

(35) *What$_i$ did you wonder [how$_j$ I repaired t$_i$ t$_j$]

(37) *[Which books]$_i$ did you wonder [to which students]$_j$ to ask [whether to give t$_i$ t$_j$]

And certainly, there is no proposal that draws together all of these residual problems.

Now consider the theory proposed here. There is one difference between Ns and Vs that follows from the basic statement of the theory and does not need to be stipulated: namely, that Vs are never addressed, because they are never visible in the sense of Chomsky (1981, 1986b), whereas we can assume that if an NP is visible and hence addressed, its address percolates to its head N. If so, then the basic difference between Ns and Vs with respect to Locality is that Vs (which have no address of their own) can be included in address-based sequences, whereas Ns (which do in general have an address of their own) cannot. Consider the structure relevant for complex NP island violations like (33), as in (124).

(124)

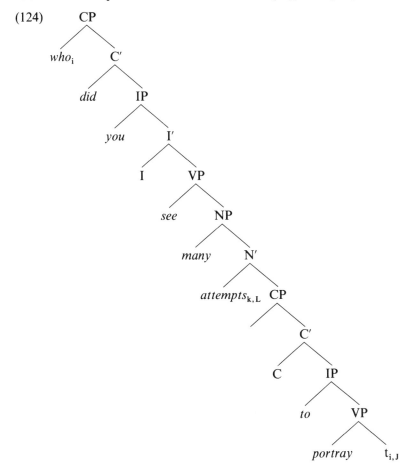

Suppose first that the *wh*-phrase in (33) moves by forming a categorial index dependency. If so, it can move as high as the embedded Spec of CP in (124), but not higher. Indeed, we can adopt the standard assumption that NP is not associated with any Ā-Spec or adjoined position; if so, a categorial index dependency must bypass NP, creating a government violation. Since adjuncts can only form categorial index dependencies, this accounts for the impossibility of extracting adjuncts not only from complex NPs, but also from NPs in general, as in (34). Suppose on the other hand that the argument in (33) moves by forming an address-based dependency. Suppose further that this dependency includes the embedded V, I, and C heads in (124); crucially, it cannot include the N head, *attempts*, since this already has an address of its own. If so, the next head that can enter the dependency is the matrix V; but this means that government is violated, since NP is once more bypassed. Thus, the impossibility of extracting an argument from complex NP islands follows, as desired.

As noted by T. Hoekstra (personal communication), this approach to islands involving N can be generalized to those involving Tense, as in (35), and those involving Determiners, as in (36), if we assume that T and D are heads. In particular, if the denoting properties of T and (definite) D are sufficient to individuate them as arguments, then T and D will be subject to the θ-Criterion and the Visibility Condition of Chomsky (1981, 1986b); hence, some (appropriately abstract form of) θ-marking and Case marking will apply to them. If so, T and (definite) D will have addresses of their own and will therefore also block address-based dependencies.

These and other predictions of the theory I am proposing are examined in detail in chapters 2 and 3. In general, however, the difference between Ns (or Ds or Ts) and Vs is just the difference between elements assigned a (visible) position and elements that assign a (visible) position; no other difference is stated in the theory. If this is correct, then the theory proposed here is superior to its competitors, which must stipulate the differences between V- and N-type heads with respect to extractions.

Furthermore, nothing in the discussion so far implies that T blocks categorial index dependencies as well as address-based dependencies. Hence, extraction across T is predicted to be possible via the formation of a categorial index sequence. But suppose that the formation of a categorial index sequence is blocked by a *wh*-island; then extraction across T is predicted to be impossible. Thus, we derive the interaction between T and *wh*-islands, as in (35). In general, it is a property of the theory proposed here that at most two Ā-extraction paths can be defined on any given subtree. One is the extraction path defined by a categorial index dependency;

Table 1.4
Island predictions an adequate theory must make

	Categorial index dependency	Address-based dependency
Subject island	*	*
Adjunct island	*	*
Relative clause island	*	*
(Complex) NP island	*	*
Definiteness island	*	*
Overlapping *wh*-islands	*	*
Wh-island	*	OK
Inner island	*	OK
Pseudo-opacity island	*	OK
Factive island	*	OK
Tense island	OK	*

the other is the extraction path defined by an address-based dependency. Hence, the theory also predicts that two extraction paths can overlap, provided one is address-based; but a third extraction path cannot overlap with them, deriving the difference between double and triple *wh*-extractions, as in (37). Thus, the theory once more predicts behaviors that other approaches can at best handle by stipulation.

I conclude this chapter by summarizing the predictions an adequate theory should make, as shown in table 1.4. Islands are grouped according to whether they give rise to violations with all dependencies, only with categorial index dependencies, or only with address-based dependencies. Whether or not the proposed theory does indeed yield the desired predictions is the crucial question that will occupy the rest of this book.

Chapter 2
Locality Theory for Movement

2.1 Subjacency

As the first step in formulating my theory, I argue (as in Manzini 1988) for a simplified version of Chomsky's (1986a) Subjacency Condition, under which the crossing of just one barrier, rather than two, counts as a violation. If this is correct, then the inheritance clause in the definition of barrierhood becomes unnecessary. Furthermore, the exceptional status of IP with respect to both barrierhood and adjunction can and must be eliminated. Thus, the definition of barrier can be simplified to (1)—that is, to Chomsky's (1986a) definition of inherent barrier or blocking category (BC). Subjacency itself can be reformulated as in (2), and the sole condition on adjunction that remains is (3).

(1) β is a barrier for α iff β is a maximal projection, β dominates α, and β is not L-marked.

(2) *Subjacency*
If α is a trace, there is an antecedent β for α such that there is no barrier for α that excludes β.

(3) An argument cannot be adjoined to.

In reducing the definition of barrier to that of BC and in defining a Subjacency violation in terms of the crossing of just one barrier, the theory in (1)–(2) essentially reverts to Huang's (1982) CED. Interestingly, Chomsky (1986a) remarks that Subjacency can refer to one versus more than one barrier, because this amounts to referring to adjacent domains (separated by one barrier) versus nonadjacent domains; but no condition can refer to a number of barriers greater than one. The antecedent government clause of the ECP can then be construed as opposing the notion of a single domain (containing no barriers) to the notion of more than one domain. Under the version of Subjacency in (2), contrary to Chomsky's (1986a) version, the latter formulation can substitute for the former, thus simplifying the grammar. The conceptual desirability of switching from what amounted to a two-barrier formulation of Subjacency in Chomsky 1973 to a one-barrier definition was in fact advocated as early as Koster 1978.

The predictions of the theory in (1)–(3) are easily checked. First consider subject islands. Subject island violations are illustrated by examples like (4), with corresponding structures like (5), where we assume that the *wh*-phrase being extracted has successfully reached the Spec of the embedded CP, α.

(4) *What$_i$ does [repairing t$_i$] bother you

(5)

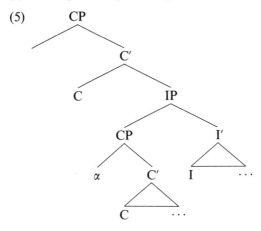

Under Chomsky's (1986a) definition, the lower CP in (5) is not L-marked, since it is not sister to a lexical head. Under (1), the lower CP is then a barrier for α; and movement of α out of the lower CP, a barrier, is blocked by Subjacency under the one-barrier formulation in (2). Adjunction to the lower CP is of course impossible under assumption (3), that arguments cannot be adjoined to. Furthermore, this version of the theory requires no stipulation concerning adjunction to IP; if α adjoins to the higher IP in (5), it still violates Subjacency, in that it crosses one barrier, the lower CP. Thus, although with respect to subject island violations the one-barrier version of Subjacency is empirically equivalent to Chomsky's (1986a) two-barrier version, it does appear to produce an overall simplification of the grammar.

Next consider adjunct island violations, as illustrated in (6). If Chomsky (1986a) is correct, adjunct sentences are attached under IP. A possible alternative, however, is to attach them under VP. Examples like (6) thus correspond to structures like (7), where both possible attachments of the adjunct CP are indicated. As before, it is assumed that the *wh*-phrase being extracted, α, has successfully reached the embedded Spec of CP position.

(6) *What$_i$ was Mary bothered [because you repaired t$_i$]

(7)

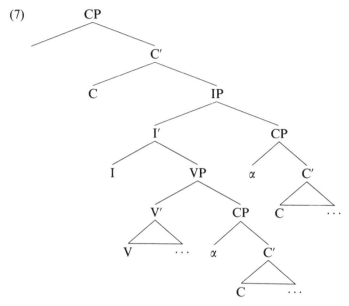

In (7) neither of the embedded CPs is L-marked, since neither is sister to a lexical head. Hence, each CP is a barrier for α under (1), and movement of α out of CP is blocked by Subjacency under the one-barrier formulation in (2). By contrast, as Chomsky (1986a) notes, the two-barrier formulation cannot predict adjunct island violations if adjuncts are attached under VP: if the adjunct CP is attached under VP, it is a barrier for α as before, but the next higher potential barrier, VP, can be circumvented by adjoining to it. Thus, given a two-barrier Subjacency, adjunct island violations can only be derived if CP is generated under IP, and even so, the assumption that adjunction to IP is impossible is crucial. In general, it appears that under the one-barrier version of Subjacency, the predictions concerning adjunct islands rest solely on the assumption that adjuncts are not sisters to heads, whereas they rest on a number of other assumptions under the two-barrier version. Again, leaving aside potential empirical problems, the one-barrier version appears to lead to a considerable simplification of the grammar. Similarly, notice that in (7) we have assumed that adjuncts are daughters of some maximal projection, IP or VP. If they are adjoined

to IP or VP, then again a one-barrier formulation of Subjacency can
predict adjunct islands, since the adjunct CP itself is a barrier. But a
two-barrier formulation fails, no matter whether the adjunct CP is adjoined to IP or VP, since by hypothesis IP and VP do not dominate CP
and hence cannot inherit barrierhood from it.

Now consider complex NP island violations, typically illustrated by
examples like (8), where an extraction takes place out of a relative clause.
The question immediately arises where relative clauses are attached. For
our purposes it suffices to assume that they are generated essentially in the
same place as adjuncts, say, as daughters to NP. If so, the structure
corresponding to (8) is (9); α in the Spec of the embedded CP again
represents the position successfully reached by the *wh*-phrase being
extracted.

(8) *What$_i$ do you know [the girl [that repaired t$_i$]]

(9)

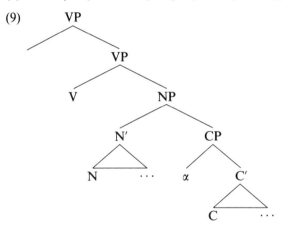

In (9) the relative clause, CP, is not L-marked, since it is not sister to a
lexical head. CP then is a barrier for α under (1), and α cannot be extracted
out of CP without violating Subjacency, as formulated in (2). In this
case Chomsky's (1986a) two-barrier formulation is also unproblematic.
Notice, however, that the same general considerations apply here as in
the case of adjuncts. Thus, suppose that the relative clause, CP, is adjoined
to NP, rather than a daughter to it. If so, NP is not a barrier by inheritance from CP, because NP does not dominate CP, and only one barrier,
CP itself, is crossed by movement to the next possible landing site, the
matrix VP-adjoined position. This leads to an incorrect prediction under
the two-barrier version of Subjacency, though not under the one-barrier
version.

Unfortunately, the one-barrier version of Subjacency shares a number of empirical problems with the two-barrier version. For instance, examples where extraction apparently takes place out of a sentential complement of an N, as in (10), have also been considered as cases of complex NP island violations. On the assumption that CP is indeed sister to N, the structure corresponding to (10) is (11).

(10) *What$_i$ did you see [many attempts [to portray t$_i$]]

(11)

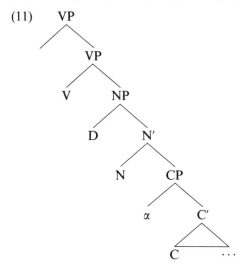

In (11) α does not cross any barriers, either inherent or by inheritance, on its way to the matrix VP-adjoined position, since CP and NP are both L-marked and hence not barriers. Thus, both the one-barrier version of Subjacency and Chomsky's (1986a) two-barrier version incorrectly predict the well-formedness of examples like (10).

In principle, we could solve this problem by assuming that the structure for complex NP island violations is never (11), but always (9), whether a relative clause is involved or not—in other words, by claiming that the CP that has been assumed to be an object of N in examples like (10) is in fact an adjunct of some sort. If so, extraction from such a CP would be blocked on the same grounds as extraction from a relative clause or an adjunct. However, Stowell (1981), who introduces the idea that apparent sentential complements of N can be appositives, distinguishes two classes of nominals that have fundamentally different properties in this respect. Although embedded sentences like (12) indeed display appositive interpretation, embedded sentences like (10) display the same interpretive relation to the head N as to the corresponding V.

(12) *Who$_i$ did you believe [claims [that they portrayed t$_i$]]

Thus, if we follow Stowell (1981), the ill-formedness of (12) can indeed be predicted on the basis of a structure like (9), but (10) must be associated with a structure like (11) as before.

The only other solution that is currently available for the problem in (10) is based on Kayne's (1981a) proposal that Vs and Ns have different properties with respect to (head) government. In particular, Cinque (1991) essentially stipulates that N does not qualify as an L-marker. If so, of course, CP in (11) is a barrier, and movement from the position of α is correctly excluded under any version of Subjacency. But such a solution is merely stipulative; rather than genuinely solving the problem, it simply restates the facts at a suitably abstract level.

At this point, it remains to ask whether the version of Subjacency in (2) correctly derives well-formed cases of extraction. Consider a typical case like (13), where movement takes place from inside an object CP. The crucial portion of the structure corresponding to (13) is shown in (14).

(13) What$_i$ do you believe [you can repair t$_i$]

(14)

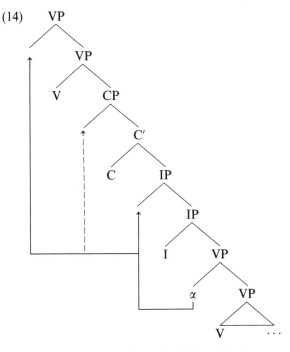

Assuming that the *wh*-phrase in (13) originally moves from the embedded object position, adjunction to the embedded VP, as in (14), neutralizes the

VP barrier, as required by (2). IP, also a barrier, can likewise be neutralized by adjunction. CP, however, is not a barrier because it is L-marked; hence, under (2) movement can successfully take place to the Spec of CP position, or directly to the next VP-adjoined one.

Interestingly, both Chomsky's (1986a) version of Subjacency and the one in (2) correctly predict the well-formedness of extraction from *wh*-islands, as in (15), as a variant of the well-formedness of sentences like (13).

(15) What$_i$ do you wonder [how$_j$ to repair t$_i$ t$_j$]

Suppose that the Spec of the embedded CP in (14) is already filled by a *wh*-phrase, so that α cannot move to it. Under the version of Subjacency in (2) there is still a perfectly well-formed derivation in which movement takes place from the embedded IP-adjoined position to the matrix VP-adjoined position; this movement crosses no barriers, since CP is not one. Similarly, under Chomsky's (1986a) version of Subjacency, movement from VP-adjoined position to VP-adjoined position in (14) crosses only one barrier, CP; indeed, IP is not an inherent barrier, and CP only inherits barrierhood from it.

However, as Chomsky (1986a) observes on the basis of Rizzi's (1980) discussion of Italian, extractions from *wh*-islands appear to interact in this case with Tense; hence, extraction from tensed *wh*-islands, as in (16), is systematically worse than extraction from untensed *wh*-islands, as in (15).

(16) *What$_i$ do you wonder [how$_j$ Mary repaired t$_i$ t$_j$]

As far as I can see, the one-barrier version of Subjacency offers no solution for this contrast equivalent to the one proposed by Chomsky (1986a). Chomsky's solution amounts to stating that a tensed IP is a barrier inherently; hence, given that CP is a barrier by inheritance, either movement takes place through the Spec of CP position, as it can do in the absence of a *wh*-island, or else two barriers, IP and CP, are crossed. In the system proposed here, IP is always a barrier, and it can furthermore always be circumvented by adjunction; moreover, an L-marked CP is never a barrier. Changing any of these assumptions, so that tensed IP or tensed CP can become an (insurmountable) barrier, has the effect of blocking any extraction out of a tensed sentence even in the absence of a *wh*-island. Hence, this system appears to be much less flexible than Chomsky's (1986a). However, Chomsky simply stipulates the properties of tensed IP. Thus, in the absence of any stipulation, the contrast between (15) and (16) seems to represent yet another problem for both versions of Subjacency.

Empirically, then, Chomsky's (1986a) version of Subjacency and the version in (2) are roughly equivalent, in terms of problems as well as solutions. The advantage of the one-barrier version is its simplicity, since it entirely dispenses with certain stipulations concerning IP that the two-barrier version must make. This is essentially the conclusion reached in Manzini 1988; similar conclusions concerning IP have also been reached on completely independent grounds by Lasnik and Saito (1992).

2.2 Antecedent Government

Now consider the ECP. Adjuncts, which do not satisfy the θ-government clause of Chomsky's (1986a) ECP and must therefore satisfy the antecedent government clause, typically display more restrictive locality patterns than arguments. In particular, like arguments, adjuncts can be extracted long-distance, as in (17); but unlike arguments, they do give rise to strong *wh*-island violations, as in (18).

(17)   How$_i$ do you believe [you can repair it t$_i$]

(18)   *How$_i$ do you wonder [what$_j$ to repair t$_j$ t$_i$]

As the next step in the discussion, I will argue (again as in Manzini 1988) that of the two notions of barrier that enter into antecedent government according to Chomsky (1986a), only one is necessary: essentially the minimality notion, which does not enter into Subjacency. Indeed, since the theory proposed here assumes that Subjacency, like antecedent government, is violated when just one barrier is crossed, Subjacency and antecedent government cannot be distinguished in terms of the number of barriers crossed. They can only be distinguished if a different definition of barrier is relevant for each.

Under the simplest conceivable definition, a barrier for a given element is a maximal projection that dominates it. This definition is sufficient to predict that adjunctions can serve as escape hatches. Consider for instance the structure in (19), relevant for (17) or (18), where the element being extracted is assumed to have reached the embedded VP-adjoined position α_1. VP is not a barrier for α_1 for the simple reason that it does not dominate it. On the other hand, IP, a maximal projection that dominates α_1, is a barrier for it. But movement can take place from α_1 to the IP-adjoined position α_2, which is not excluded by IP, so that IP is not technically crossed.

(19)

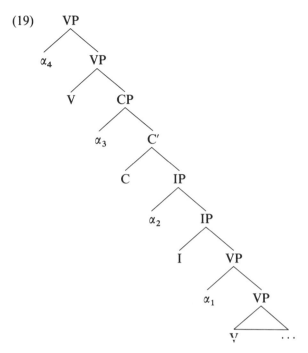

On the other hand, defining a barrier for some given element as the first maximal projection that dominates it is not sufficient to predict that a Spec position, and in particular the Spec of CP position, can also be an escape hatch for it. Thus, suppose that from the IP-adjoined position α_2 in (19) movement takes place to the Spec of CP position, α_3, since adjunction to the argument CP is prohibited under (3). If a barrier for α is simply the first maximal projection that dominates α, then CP is a barrier for α_3 and movement to the next possible landing site, α_4, is impossible because it crosses CP. This of course incorrectly blocks all well-formed extractions like (17).

In general, then, we want a maximal projection not to be a barrier for its Spec. Now, according to a modified definition of L-marking proposed by Chomsky (1986a), the Spec position of an XP is L-marked just in case XP itself is. Technically, a maximal projection is taken to agree with both its head and its Spec, as in (20).

(20) A maximal projection agrees with its head and its Spec.

Furthermore, L-marking is defined to hold between a lexical head and a maximal projection XP that it θ-governs, or between the lexical head and those positions that XP agrees with, as in (21).

(21) β L-marks α iff β is lexical and
   a. β θ-governs α or
   b. β θ-governs γ and γ agrees with α.

This means that L-marking holds between a lexical head and the Spec or head of a maximal projection that it θ-governs. For instance, in (19) V L-marks not just CP, but also C and the Spec of CP α_3.

Suppose we formulate a notion of *g (overnment)-marking* that is like the notion of L-marking in (21) in that it holds of a head and a maximal projection, or the head or the Spec of the maximal projection. Crucially, however, g-marking differs from the basic definition of L-marking, as well as from (21), in that it does not refer to lexicality. It also finally abandons the notion of θ-government in favor of the weaker notion of sisterhood to a head, since the stronger notion does not appear to have any motivation within the theory proposed here. G-marking is thus defined as follows:

(22) β g-marks α iff β is a head and
   a. β is a sister to α or
   b. β is a sister to a category that agrees with α.

Under (22), since the Spec of CP is g-marked by any head sister to CP, α_3 is g-marked by V in (19). Suppose we say, then, that a (government) barrier for a g-marked element is any maximal projection that dominates it and its g-marker, as in (23).

(23) β is a barrier for α iff β is a maximal projection, β dominates α, and if α is g-marked, β dominates the g-marker of α.

If α_3 is g-marked by V in (19), then CP is not a barrier for α_3 because it does not dominate the g-marker for α_3, V. It follows that movement of α_3 can take place across CP to the next landing site, α_4; in other words, the Spec of CP is an escape hatch, as desired. On the other hand, under (23) a barrier for a non-g-marked element is simply any maximal projection that dominates it; this ensures that government barriers are defined for non-g-marked elements as well.

Let us return to (17)–(18). If we assume Chomsky's (1986a) ECP, then movement of an object, as in (13) and (15), always satisfies the ECP by θ-government. It then remains to check whether the theory in (22)–(23) yields the desired results for non-θ-governed elements, as in (17)–(18), assuming that (22)–(23) define the notion of barrier for antecedent government. If the adjunct in (17) is generated under VP, then the structure relevant for (17) is again (19). Movement from a VP-internal position to the VP-adjoined position α_1 is obviously successful; VP is a barrier for a

VP-internal position, but the VP-adjoined position α_1 is not excluded by VP and thus government is satisfied. Once the adjunct is in α_1, IP is a barrier for it; but again movement can take place to the IP-adjoined position, α_2, without crossing the IP barrier and hence without violating government. CP in turn is a barrier for α_2, but movement to the Spec of CP position, α_3, does not cross CP and therefore satisfies government. Finally, CP is not a barrier for its Spec α_3 under the new definitions in (22)–(23) since α_3 is g-marked by V from outside CP; hence, movement can successfully take place to the next VP-adjoined position, α_4. Thus, (22)–(23) make possible a derivation for well-formed adjunct extraction examples like (17).

Crucially, in order for (22)–(23) to be empirically adequate as components of a theory of antecedent government, the ill-formedness of *wh*-island violations with adjuncts, as in (18), should also follow from them. Under this theory, extraction can proceed as in (17) to the α_2 position in (19). Movement to the Spec of CP position α_3 is then blocked by the presence of another *wh*-phrase. Hence, movement can only take place from α_2 to the next landing site, α_4. But this in turn means that CP, a barrier for α_2, is crossed and the antecedent government clause of the ECP is violated. It follows that (22)–(23) correctly predict examples like (18) to be ill formed.

The next question concerns the status of subjects under extraction. Clearly, objects are θ-governed and adjuncts are not. In which of these classes do subjects fall? Relevant counterparts to (17) and (18) with subjects are shown in (24) and (25). (24) is well formed, on a par with (17); the *wh*-island violation (25) is ill formed, on a par with (18). The violation in (25) is judged to be strong, comparable to the violation in (18).

(24)   Who$_i$ do you believe [t$_i$ is a painter]

(25)   *Who$_i$ do you wonder [what$_j$ t$_i$ painted t$_j$]

The relevant structure for extraction is again (19), though the subject of course originates in the Spec of IP position. Under (23), IP is not a barrier for its Spec position, which is g-marked by C. Hence, movement of the subject from the Spec of IP position to the Spec of CP position α_3 in (19) is well formed under antecedent government, whether it passes through the IP-adjoined position α_2 or not. Similarly, movement from the Spec of CP position α_3 to the next available landing site, the VP-adjoined position α_4, is well formed under antecedent government. However, movement from the Spec of IP position to the matrix VP-adjoined position α_4 crosses a barrier, CP, and therefore violates government even if it passes through the IP-adjoined position α_2. Thus, antecedent government correctly predicts the contrast between (24), where the embedded Spec of CP is not filled, allowing the subject to move through it, and (25), where movement of the subject through the embedded Spec of CP is blocked by the presence of another *wh*-phrase. This in turn apparently means that subjects must satisfy the antecedent government clause of the ECP, like adjuncts and unlike objects; in other words, they cannot satisfy θ-government. The latter conclusion correctly follows from Chomsky's (1986a) definition of θ-government, since the subject is not θ-marked by a head.

However, in another respect the extraction of subjects patterns against the extraction of both adjuncts and objects. Objects and adjuncts are insensitive to whether the C position is empty or filled, as in (26)–(27); by contrast, subjects can be extracted across an empty C, as in (24), but not across a lexical C, as in (28).

(26)   What$_i$ do you believe [(that) Mary painted t$_i$]

(27)   How$_i$ do you believe [(that) Mary painted it t$_i$]

(28)   *Who$_i$ do you believe [that t$_i$ is a painter]

Obviously, the theory correctly predicts the well-formed examples with objects and adjuncts. θ-governed elements such as objects can cross any CP altogether; non-θ-governed elements, such as adjuncts, must pass through the Spec of CP position, but nothing in the discussion so far blocks this possibility if C is lexically filled.

In Chomsky 1986a the ill-formedness of (28)—more generally, the *That-t* Filter—follows from the minimality notion of barrier. But the notion of barrier defined for antecedent government in (22)–(23) is essentially Chomsky's (1986a) minimality. In particular, under (22), any head β g-marks into the Spec and head of a maximal projection α that it is a sister to; however, g-marking never proceeds beyond the head of α. Thus, it is the head of α itself that can be construed as blocking g-marking. If so, to the extent that g-marking is built into the definition of barrier in (23), government is again blocked by a head. To fully adopt Chomsky's (1986a) notion of minimality into our theory, we simply need to say that given an element α and a g-marker for it, β, a one-bar projection of β is also a barrier for α, provided additionally that β is lexically realized.

Consider once again the structure in (19). Movement from α_1 to α_2 is well formed as before because IP is not crossed and I′ is always defective with respect to barrierhood, accepting Chomsky's (1986a) theory in this respect. By hypothesis, movement from α_2 to α_3 is well formed if C is not lexical, but not if C is lexical, because in the latter case the C' barrier is crossed; CP is not crossed in either case. Finally, movement from α_3 to α_4 is well formed if we assume with Chomsky (1986a) that V' is not expanded in the absence of the Spec of VP; as before, VP is not crossed.

Unfortunately, this translation of Chomsky's (1986a) solution to the *that-t* phenomenon into the theory I am proposing appears to have all the unappealing properties of the original and more. Within the theory proposed here, indeed, the fact that the exceptional character of I' must be stipulated reduces the gains to be had from the one-barrier definition of Subjacency. To this must be added the doubtful assumption that V' is not expanded in the absence of a Spec of VP. If the absence of the Spec of VP is a general property, then it creates an asymmetry in the theory; if it is not a general property, then a potential empirical problem arises.

To sum up: So far I have argued that just as Chomsky's (1986a) two-barrier Subjacency can be reduced to a one-barrier version without loss of predictive power and with a gain in simplicity, so the two notions of barrier that enter into Chomsky's (1986a) antecedent government can be reduced to one, essentially the minimality notion, as in (22)–(23). Again this result can be achieved without any loss of empirical predictions, though at the cost of some enrichment of the theory, comparable to Chomsky's (1986a) in the case of *that-t* phenomena.

Now consider Subjacency again. Subjacency predicts essentially three types of violations: subject islands, adjunct islands, and complex NP (relative clause) islands. It is easy to show that these same violations are predicted by the antecedent government clause of the ECP for those elements that are subject to it, namely, non-θ-governed elements. Consider for instance subject islands, as in (29).

(29) *How$_i$ does [repairing it t$_i$] bother you

The relevant configuration is as in (5), where it is assumed that the phrase being extracted, α, has reached the Spec of the embedded CP.

In (5) α does not have a g-marker, since the embedded CP is not sister to a head and g-marking therefore does not extend to its Spec. The embedded CP then is a government barrier for α, since it is a maximal projection that dominates it. It follows that if α moves to the next possible landing site, an IP-adjoined position, it crosses a government barrier, the embedded CP, and it violates the antecedent government clause of the ECP. But if movement of α out of the configuration in (5) violates the antecedent government clause of the ECP, then the ECP in general predicts subject islands for all and only the elements to which antecedent government applies. Thus, Subjacency is needed only to predict the behavior of θ-governed elements and is otherwise derivable from the ECP.

Similar considerations apply to adjunct islands, as in (30).

(30) *How$_i$ was Mary bothered [because you repaired it t$_i$]

The relevant configuration is given in (7), where the phrase being extracted, α, has reached the Spec position of the adjunct CP. Again, α is not g-marked; hence, the adjunct CP is a government barrier for α, since CP is a maximal projection that dominates α. The next possible landing site for α is an IP-adjoined position. Movement of α to this position crosses a government barrier, the adjunct CP, and is therefore blocked by the antecedent government clause of the ECP. Incidentally, the same conclusion holds if adjuncts are attached under VP; in this case it is sufficient to substitute VP for IP in the preceding discussion. As before, however, the antecedent government clause of the ECP applies only to non-θ-governed elements. Hence, the ECP can predict adjunct islands, as in (7), only for non-θ-governed elements. For θ-governed elements, not subject to antecedent government, Subjacency is still required.

The same conclusion holds for complex NP islands, as in (31).

(31) *How$_i$ do you know [the girl [that repaired it t$_i$]]

The relevant configuration is given in (9); as before, the phrase being extracted, α, has reached the Spec position of the embedded CP, a relative clause. CP is a government barrier for α, since α is not g-marked and CP is a maximal projection that dominates it. Since the next available landing site for α is a VP-adjoined position, it follows that movement of α crosses a government barrier, CP, and therefore violates the antecedent government clause of the ECP. Hence, if α is not θ-governed, the island violation is predicted by the ECP. Subjacency is needed only to predict a violation in case α is θ-governed and therefore not subject to antecedent government.

More interestingly, antecedent government subsumes not only subject, adjunct, and relative clause islands violations, which are accounted for by Subjacency, but also complex NP island violations where extraction takes place from a complement of N, as in (32), which are not.

(32) *How$_i$ did you see [many attempts [to portray Mary t$_i$]]

The corresponding configuration is given in (11), where the adjunct being extracted, α, has reached the embedded Spec of CP position. CP is not a barrier for α, because N g-marks α from outside CP. However, very much for the same reason, NP is a barrier for α. Suppose, then, that we adopt the common assumption that no $\bar{A}$-Spec is available within NP. Of course, α cannot adjoin to NP, because NP is an argument; hence, it is forced to move to the next landing site, a VP-adjoined position. But this means that α crosses the NP barrier, and antecedent government predicts that the construction is ill formed.

In summary, for each of the major island configurations in (29), (30), and (31), as well as for the problematic island configuration in (32), we have seen that the antecedent government clause of the ECP predicts the relevant violations. This means of course that with respect to non-θ-governed elements, Subjacency itself is derivable from the ECP. Apparently then, Subjacency reduces to a requirement on θ-governed elements. This revised Subjacency can be expressed as in (33), where "α is subjacent to β" means that there must be no barrier for α, in the sense defined by (1), that excludes β.

(33) *Subjacency*
    If α is a trace and α is θ-governed, there is an antecedent β for α such that α is subjacent to β.

On the other hand, the real content of the ECP appears to be expressed by its antecedent government clause. The θ-government clause does not express any restriction; to all intents and purposes, it simply exempts θ-governed elements from the antecedent government requirement. Thus, the real content of the ECP reduces to something like (34), where government is understood exactly as in Chomsky 1986a, except for being defined in terms of the notion of barrier in (22)–(23).

(34) *ECP*
    If α is a trace and α is not θ-governed, there is an antecedent β for α such that β governs α.

The drawback of this theory is obvious. The conceptual core of Chomsky's (1986a) theory, and the reason I have chosen it as a basis for discussion, in preference to available alternatives, is that it at least partially unifies Subjacency and the antecedent government clause of the ECP, via the notion of barrier that the two share. In the system I have proposed, Subjacency and the ECP, though each potentially simplified when considered in itself, once more become two entirely disjoint principles. Indeed, under (33)–(34), Subjacency and the ECP not only employ different notions of locality, but also apply to different sets of elements. The question, then, is whether this double disjunction can be (partially) reduced without sacrificing the theoretical simplifications that have otherwise been achieved.

2.3   Unification of Subjacency and Antecedent Government

Suppose that, following Manzini (1988), we take the step of collapsing Subjacency and the ECP as they now stand in (33)–(34). The result is the extension of the ECP in (35). Under (35), neither the disjunction between Subjacency and the antecedent government clause of the ECP, nor the ECP-internal disjunction between θ-governed and non θ-governed elements is resolved, though the two disjunctions are seen to pattern together.

(35) *ECP*
   If α is a trace, there is an antecedent β for α such that
   a. α is θ-governed and α is subjacent to β; or
   b. β governs α.

In (35) the conditions on θ-governed and non-θ-governed elements are formally identical. However, through the notions "subjacent to" and "governed by," they refer to two different notions of barrier, as in (1) and (23), respectively. An attempt at unifying the disjunction in (35) can then start with the two different notions of barrier. These do not differ substantially with respect to the primitive notions they employ; the only difference in this respect seems to be that the notion of lexicality is relevant for Subjacency barriers through the notion of L-marking in (21), but not for government barriers, which employ the simplified notion of g-marking in (22).

There is at least one reason why, in attempting to reduce one notion of barrier to the other, the notion of government barrier can be considered the more likely candidate for success. As we have seen, the notion of Subjacency barrier faces a number of empirical problems. By contrast, the notion of government barrier has as much empirical success with subject, adjunct, and complex NP islands involving relative clauses as the notion of Subjacency barrier itself; in addition, it can account for complex NP islands involving sentential complements of N, as in (32), which the notion of Subjacency barrier cannot handle.

Consider the L-marking requirement, by which Subjacency barriers differ from government barriers. Under the core definition, an element is L-marked just in case it is a sister to a lexical head. The agreement part of the definition of L-marking, as in (21), was crucially incorporated into the notion of g-marking; but in predicting all of the Subjacency data considered so far, it was not actually used.

In turn, there is one and only one reason why the notion of lexicality is crucial in the definition of L-marking. Suppose we take sisterhood to a head as the relevant property for the definition of L-marking. Subjects still turn out to be islands, because they are clearly not sisters to a head. So do adjuncts, and so do relative clauses. Hence, all fundamental island violations can still be derived. Similarly, objects are not islands because by definition they are sisters to a head. The only effect of the lexicality requirement is to ensure that VP and IP are also barriers. Without this requirement, VP and IP would not be barriers, since they are sisters to heads—I and C, respectively—though nonlexical ones. The fact that VP and IP are barriers is in turn the only property of the theory that ensures that movement is successive cyclic under Subjacency. Thus, the notion of L-marking can be reduced to that of sisterhood to a head as long as we are willing to give up the idea that movement is necessarily successive cyclic.

Suppose we carry out the suggested reduction. Then the first clause of the ECP in (35) reduces to the statement that if a trace is θ-governed, there is no maximal projection intervening between it and its antecedent that is not sister to a head. In other words, all the maximal projections intervening between the trace and its antecedent must be sisters to a head. Notice that given a maximal projection XP that is sister to a head Y, the head and Spec of XP are g-marked by Y under (22); hence, XP is not a government barrier for them under (23). By contrast, given a maximal projection XP that is not sister to a head, its head and Spec are not g-marked; hence, XP is a barrier for them. Thus, the requirement that XP must be sister to a head can be replaced by the requirement that there must be an XP-internal position and an XP-external position that are in a government relation.

Next let us consider the first clause of the ECP in (35). If the preceding argument is correct, this clause can be reduced to the statement that for each maximal projection XP intervening between a θ-governed trace and an antecedent for it, there must be two positions, one internal and one external to XP, that are in a government relation. The advantage of such a formulation, as in (36), is that both clauses of the ECP, the first of which subsumes Subjacency, now refer to the same notion of locality—namely, government. Thus, (36) finally represents a degree of unification of locality comparable to that achieved under Chomsky's (1986a) theory.

(36) *ECP*

    If α is a trace, there is an antecedent β for α such that

    a. α is θ-governed and for each maximal projection XP that dominates α and excludes β there is a position dominated by XP, γ, and a position excluded by XP, γ', such that γ' governs γ; or

    b. β governs α.

Under (36), the real difference between the two clauses of the ECP, or Subjacency and the antecedent government clause of the ECP, is that one clause requires government to hold of each link of a chain, and the other requires government to hold of random pairs of positions. The most immediate drawback of (36) is that no good definition appears to be available for the theoretical construct involved in the latter requirement. Let us try to provide one. In representational terms, at the most basic level a chain is simply an ordered set of positions, where the ordering is provided by c-command. Suppose we introduce an independent definition for the notion of a set of positions ordered by c-command; we can call this construct, underlying the notion of chain, a *c-(command) set*, as in (37).

(37) $(\alpha_1, \ldots, \alpha_n)$ is a c-(command) set iff for all i, α_i c-commands α_{i+1}.

The idea is that although the notion of chain defines one construct relevant for the satisfaction of ECP, the alternative construct is defined simply by the notion of c-set. In other words, given a trace and an antecedent for it, the ECP translates into the requirement that either the antecedent governs the trace, or else there is a c-set, connecting the trace and its antecedent, that satisfies government. The more stringent requirement applies when the trace is not θ-governed, the less stringent requirement when the trace is θ-governed. Government is in turn said to be satisfied by a c-set just in case for every member α_i of the c-set, α_i governs α_{i+1}. Thus, we arrive at the revision of (35) in (38)–(39).

(38) $(\alpha_1, \ldots, \alpha_n)$ satisfies government iff for all i, α_i governs α_{i+1}.

(39) *ECP*

    If α is a trace, there is an antecedent β for α such that

    a. α is θ-governed and there is a c-(command) set $(\beta, \ldots, \alpha)$ that satisfies government; or

    b. (β, α) satisfies government.

In summary, in (39), as in (35) and (36), the disjunction between the ECP and Subjacency is reabsorbed under the original ECP-internal disjunction between θ-government and antecedent government. In (39), furthermore, as in (36), the two clauses of the disjunction are formulated in terms of the same definition of locality—government. At this point it remains only to test the predictions of the new theory systematically, retracing our steps to the relevant examples. The positions from which extraction can take place, adjoined positions aside, are as in (40), where α_3 is taken to be the adjunct position. In (40) the embedded CP is represented as the object of the matrix V.

(40)

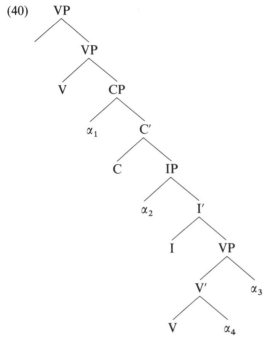

First consider the embedded object, α_4 in (40). If α_4 is to form a chain that satisfies government, it must be moved to a VP-adjoined position, then to an IP-adjoined position, and then to the Spec of CP position α_1. If the embedded CP is in object position, as in (40), it is not a barrier for α_1; hence, α_1 can move to the next VP-adjoined position, and so on. However, if the embedded CP is a subject, adjunct, or relative clause, as in (4), (6), and (8), repeated, here, then CP is a barrier for α_1 exactly as it is for α in (5), (7), and (9), respectively; hence, no movement can take place under government.

(4) *What$_i$ does [repairing t$_i$] bother you

(6) *What$_i$ was Mary bothered [because you repaired t$_i$]

(8) *What$_i$ do you know [the girl [that repaired t$_i$]]

Suppose on the other hand that α_4 moves in one step to α_1, disregarding antecedent government. Since α_4 is θ-governed by V, government can indeed be satisfied by a c-set under (39). α_4 can first form a link of a c-set with a VP-internal position for which VP is not a barrier—say, V. Government automatically holds of this (V, α_4) link. V can then form a link of a c-set with an IP-internal position—say, I. The (I, V) link also satisfies government. IP turns out not to be a government barrier for the chosen IP-internal position, I, and a link with a CP-internal position—say, (C, I) —that satisfies government can also be formed. In short, if α_4 moves in one step to α_1, there is at least one c-set—namely, $(\alpha_1, C, I, V, \alpha_4)$—that satisfies government.

Suppose now that α_4 moves not to α_1 but rather across CP—say, to the matrix VP-adjoined position. We have seen that a c-set that satisfies government can be constructed up to the embedded C head in (40). If the embedded CP is an object of V, as in (40), then it is not a barrier for C and there will be a VP-internal position—say, V itself—that governs it. Hence, a well- formed link can be added to the c-set we have constructed, yielding (V, C, I, V, α_4). Suppose, however, that the embedded CP is a subject, adjunct, or relative clause, as in (4), (6), and (8). In none of these cases is a CP-internal position g-marked from outside CP, because CP is not sister to a head. Hence CP is a barrier for any CP-internal position, and no CP-internal position can be governed from outside CP. This means that no well-formed c-set can be extended beyond the embedded C, and if it is, an ECP violation ultimately results under (39).

In short, if α_4 moves successive cyclically, then it is predicted to be sensitive to subject islands, adjunct islands, and complex NP islands under antecedent government. If α_4 moves in one step and a c-set is constructed to satisfy locality, exactly the same sensitivity to islands is predicted. The result is that (4), (6), and (8) are predicted to be ill formed under all possible derivations, as desired. Consider on the other hand *wh*-islands, to which α_4 is insensitive, as in (15), repeated here.

(15) What$_i$ do you wonder [how$_j$ to repair t$_i$ t$_j$]

If α_4 moves successive cyclically, a government violation arises because the Spec of CP position α_1 is independently filled, and movement from the embedded IP-adjoined position to the matrix VP-adjoined position in (40) crosses a barrier, the embedded CP. However, suppose that α_4 moves in one step, as it is also allowed to do. Then in (40) there is always a well-formed c-set relating α_4 to a position external to the embedded CP, of the type constructed before, $(\ldots, V, C, I, V, \alpha_4)$, which is entirely insensitive to whether the Spec of CP position is filled or not. Thus, *wh*-islands are predicted to be irrelevant for α_4, as desired.

Consider by contrast movement from a subject position (α_2 in (40)) or from an adjunct position (α_3 in (40)). The difference between an object (α_4 in (40)) and a subject or an adjunct is that the latter two are not θ-governed. Hence, they must satisfy the ECP through antecedent government; in other words, they cannot satisfy government through a c-set. If antecedent government is to be satisfied, in turn, they must move through the α_1 position, from which they can then move to a CP-external position, provided the embedded CP is itself an object, as indeed it is in (40). If CP is not an object, as in (29)–(31), repeated here, then antecedent government is violated, and subject, adjunct, and complex NP island violations are correctly predicted to arise.

(29) *How$_i$ does [repairing it t$_i$] bother you

(30) *How$_i$ was Mary bothered [because you repaired it t$_i$]

(31) *How$_i$ do you know [the girl [that repaired it t$_i$]

What is more, because subjects and adjuncts must satisfy antecedent government, which can only be satisfied if movement proceeds through the Spec of CP position, α_1, subjects and adjuncts are predicted to be sensitive to the presence of another *wh*-phrase in this position, and hence to *wh*-islands, as in (18), repeated here.

(18) *How$_i$ do you wonder [what$_j$ to repair t$_j$ t$_i$]

Thus, the crucial contrast between objects and nonobjects with respect to *wh*-island violations, as well as their similarity with respect to all other islands, follows from the ECP in (39).

Notice also that the definition of θ-government excludes any derived position, including α_1 in (40) and all adjoined positions, from being θ-governed. Hence, any intermediate trace of movement can only be licensed through antecedent government. This means that there is no position to which adjuncts or subjects can move in order to avoid satisfying antecedent government, again as desired. By contrast, if objects move to some derived position, they are forced to satisfy antecedent government from that position onward. But this is empirically irrelevant, since objects are never forced to move otherwise than in one step.

Let us draw our conclusions so far. The ECP in (39) achieves a degree of unification for Subjacency and the ECP comparable to that of Chomsky's (1986a) theory, since one definition of locality—here, government—

is relevant to both clauses of the revised ECP. The version of the theory that I have proposed accounts for subject, adjunct, and complex NP (relative clause) islands for all extractions; for nonobject extractions it additionally accounts for complex NP islands involving sentential complements of N, as in (32). Furthermore, this version of the theory correctly accounts for *wh*-island violations with nonobjects as in (18). The only residual problem is that it cannot incorporate *that-t* violations with subjects, which could be derived in Chomsky's (1986a) theory by postulating an additional definition of locality relevant for antecedent government only (namely, minimality for X' (one-bar) projections).

Before we turn to these violations, however, it is worth noting that the direction in which my theory has developed so far, essentially along the lines of Manzini 1988, brings it in contact with models other than Chomsky's (1986a). For example, Rizzi (1990) also views the two classes of movement characterized roughly by *wh*-island violations and lack of *wh*-island violations as corresponding to successive-cyclic movement and one-step movement, respectively. In this respect, one important question can immediately be laid to rest. This is the question of the empirical consequences of adopting one-step movement for an important class of extractions, given the evidence in the literature for the successive-cyclic nature of *wh*-movement in general. Consider for instance Torrego's (1984) argument that *wh*-movement must be successive cyclic in Spanish. According to Torrego (1984), Spanish has a rule that moves an auxiliary-verb complex in front of the subject when the COMP position (in present terms, the Spec of CP position) is occupied by a *wh*-phrase. Torrego (1984) notices that a trace in this position also triggers inversion, as in (41) (her (19b)).

(41) Qué$_i$ pensaba Juan [que le había dicho Pedro [que
     what did John think that had told him Peter   that
     había publicado la revista   t$_i$]]
     had published   the journal

Here *qué* moves from the most embedded object position. If it passes through each Spec of CP on its way, the multiple inversions in (41) are automatically explained.

Crucially, the counterpart to (41) without inversions in the embedded sentences is excluded, as in (42) (Torrego's (19c)).

(42) *Qué$_i$ pensaba Juan [que Pedro le había dicho [que la revista
     what did John think that Peter had told him   that the journal
     había publicado t$_i$]]
     had published

The impossibility of noninverted forms in (41) shows that *qué* not only can, but must, pass through each Spec of CP on its way to sentence-initial position. If successive-cyclic movement through the Spec of CP is not enforced, then both (41) and (42) are predicted to be possible.

In fact, Torrego's (1984) argument works in favor of rather than against the theory I am proposing. Of course, in the case of non-θ-governed elements, successive-cyclic movement through the Spec of CP is enforced under all theories by the antecedent government clause of the ECP. However, consider direct objects. Chomsky's (1986a) theory is constructed so that a direct object must move successive cyclically, but not necessarily through the Spec of CP. Indeed, in a structure like (40) it can move from VP-adjoined to VP-adjoined position, crossing at most one barrier, CP, so that Subjacency is not violated. This is crucial, if *wh*-phrases are to be allowed to move across *wh*-islands, as they must be in Spanish by Torrego's (1984) account. Under (39), on the other hand, if antecedent government is not satisfied, then government must be satisfied via a c-set. Now, in (40) government will be satisfied via a c-set only if the c-set includes some CP-internal escape hatch, hence again the Spec of CP or C. This makes it possible to straightforwardly predict Torrego's (1984) data within the theory proposed here, by stating that verb movement applies in Spanish when either the Spec of CP or its head C is a member of a *wh*-headed c-set or chain.

2.4   Head Government

We can now turn to the major residual problem for the theory I am proposing of predicting *that-t* violations with extraction from the subject position. The relevant configuration is given in (43), where α represents the subject position in the Spec of IP. The basic examples are as in (24) and (28), repeated here.

(24)   Who$_i$ do you believe [t$_i$ is a painter]

(28)   *Who$_i$ do you believe [that t$_i$ is a painter]

As already noted, no comparable violation arises with direct objects, as in (26), which suggests that the *That-t* Filter is related to antecedent government. On the other hand no *that- t* violation arises with adjuncts either, as in (27), which suggests on the contrary that the filter cannot be subsumed under antecedent government.

(26)   What$_i$ do you believe [(that) Mary painted t$_i$]

(27) How$_i$ do you believe [(that) Mary painted it t$_i$]

Remember furthermore that adjacency of the trace to *that* is crucial to the *That-t* Filter. Thus, in (44), where movement takes place from the most embedded subject position to the matrix Spec of CP across an intermediate C filled by *that*, no violation arises.

(43)

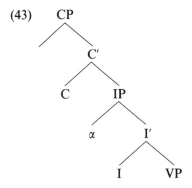

(44) Who$_i$ did you say [(that) John believes [t$_i$ is a painter]]

Examples like (44) lead to another set of data that point to the inadequacy of antecedent government, not so much in predicting *that-t* violations, as in predicting the behavior of subjects under extraction in general. In the preceding discussion, following Chomsky (1986a), we have derived *wh*-island violations with both adjuncts and subjects, as in (18) and (25), respectively, under the antecedent government clause of the ECP.

(18) *How$_i$ do you wonder [what$_j$ to repair t$_j$ t$_i$]

(25) *Who$_i$ do you wonder [what$_j$ t$_i$ painted t$_j$]

Now, under antecedent government, *wh*-island violations are predicted to arise not only in (18) and (25), but also in examples like (45) and (46), where an adjunct and a subject, respectively, are moved from a doubly embedded sentence to the matrix sentence across an intermediate *wh*-island. The intuition is that whereas (18), (25), and (45) are strongly ill formed, (46) is essentially well formed.

(45) *How$_i$ do you wonder [whether to believe [Mary repaired it t$_i$]

(46)   Who$_i$ do you wonder [whether to believe [t$_i$ is a painter]]

Examples like (18), (25), and (45)–(46), which involve question formation, can be usefully compared with examples like (47)–(50), where *wh*-extraction is used to form a relative clause.

(47) *The man [who$_i$ I wondered [what$_j$ t$_i$ painted t$_j$]] . . .

(48) *The reason [why$_i$ I wondered [what$_j$ Mary repaired t$_j$ t$_i$]] ...

(49) The man [who$_i$ I wondered [whether to believe [t$_i$ was a painter]]] ...

(50) *The reason [why$_i$ I wondered [whether to believe [Mary repaired it t$_i$]]] ...

(48) and (50), where an adjunct is extracted across a *wh*-island, are strongly ill formed independently of whether extraction site and *wh*-island are in the same sentence or one sentence apart. However, (47), where a *wh*-island is adjacent to the extraction site of a subject, is a strong violation, whereas (49) is essentially well formed.

The preceding examples point to the conclusion that antecedent government correctly predicts the behavior of adjuncts but not of subjects. The behavior of subjects instead appears to pattern essentially with that of θ-governed elements like objects, except that subjects are also sensitive to two filters, governed by adjacency or strict locality, one excluding the *that-t* configuration in (28), the other excluding a *wh-t* configuration, as in (25) or (47). In sentences where these two filters are satisfied, as in (44), (46), or (49), the extraction of subjects is sensitive only to Subjacency, exactly like the extraction of objects, and does not display any antecedent government effects, unlike the extraction of adjuncts.

These conclusions appear to be reinforced if we consider French. French has its own version of the *That-t* Filter, in that the counterpart to *that*, *que*, must agree with an adjacent subject trace, yielding *qui*. This is seen in the contrast between (51) and (52), (51) corresponding to English (28) and (52) differing from (51) in the choice of *qui* rather than *que*.

(51) *Qui penses-tu que est un peintre

(52) Qui penses-tu qui est un peintre

Contrary to what happens in English, where *that* is in free distribution with the zero C, in French *qui* can only appear adjacent to a subject extraction site, as shown for instance by its unacceptability in (53)–(54), corresponding to English (26), where an object is extracted.

(53) Qu'est-ce que tu penses que Marie a peint

(54) *Qu'est-ce que tu penses qui Marie a peint

French furthermore displays *wh-t* effects, in that a subject cannot be extracted from a site adjacent to a *wh*-island, as in (55), behaving in this respect like an adjunct, as in (56). As in English, on the other hand, an adjunct cannot be extracted from a *wh*-island one sentence removed from its extraction site, as in (57), but a similar extraction with a subject is (relatively) well formed, as in (58). (55)–(58) translate English (25), (18), (45), and (46), respectively.

(55) *Qui$_i$ te demandes-tu [quoi$_j$ t$_i$ a peint t$_j$]

(56) *Comment$_i$ te demandes-tu [quoi$_j$ réparer t$_j$ t$_i$]

(57) *Comment$_i$ te demandes-tu [si on croit [que Marie l'a réparé t$_i$]]

(58) Qui$_i$ te demandes-tu [si on croit [qui t$_i$ est un peintre]]

To repeat: The correct systematization of the data concerning subject extractions appears to be that subjects must obey both a *That-t* Filter and a *Wh-t* Filter; given that requirement, they behave like θ-governed elements under extraction. Remember also that whereas *wh-t* patterns of the type in (25) versus (46) do not follow under Chomsky's (1986a) antecedent government, *that-t* patterns, as in (24)–(28) and (44), follow under it only given the minimality notion of barrier and additional assumptions whose theoretical status remains unclear, most importantly the assumption that antecedent government must be satisfied at S-structure for A-positions, but only at LF for $\bar{\text{A}}$-positions, as proposed by Lasnik and Saito (1984). In other words, whereas the antecedent government explanation for *wh-t* effects appears to be completely ruled out on empirical grounds, the antecedent government explanation for *that-t* effects appears to have at least theoretical drawbacks.

Consider the *That-t* filter. Following Rizzi's (1990) approach, both in English and in French C must agree with an adjacent subject trace; *qui* is the agreeing form in French, whence the *que-qui* alternation, whereas a zero C, but not *that*, can be an agreeing form in English, whence the *That-t* Filter. The real question is what forces this agreement between C and an adjacent subject trace to obtain. According to Rizzi (1990), the answer lies in a notion of head government. In particular, the subject is not head-governed by I; if C does not agree with it, then it is not head-governed by C either, but if C does agree with it, then it is head-governed by C. Since the subject agrees with I, the agreement of C with the subject can in turn be viewed as taking place through agreement of C with I. If so, then the generalization underlying the *That-t* Filter is that although the subject is not head-governed by I, it is head-governed by C agreeing with I.

In order to capture this generalization, it appears that we must extend the notion of θ-government, adopted from Chomsky (1986a), to some notion of head government of the type proposed by Rizzi (1990). Of course, the original notion of θ-government involved θ-marking by, and sisterhood to, a head. But there is another relation that can obviously involve a head and a phrasal constituent—namely, Case marking, where the relevant structural configuration is much less restrictive than sisterhood, corresponding in fact to government. Suppose, then, that we define a notion of *K-government* to correspond roughly to Case marking by a head, as in (59).

(59) β K-governs α iff β is a head and β Case-marks α.

Consider again the crucial structure in (43). Under (59), if C in (43) agrees with I, and if agreement with I is taken to imply agreement with respect to the Case-marking properties of I, then C K-governs the subject α. If C does not agree with I, then of course C does not K-govern α. However, under (59) I also K-governs the subject α, since straightforwardly, it Case-marks it. Thus, the preliminary definition of K-government in (59) is inadequate to discriminate between the relation of α to I and the relation of α to agreeing C in (43). It must be refined so that α in (43) is K-governed by agreeing C but not by I.

Two obvious differences concerning the position of C and I with respect to the subject are discussed by Rizzi (1990). On the one hand, C and I are on opposite sides of α in (43). Hence, if there is a canonical government restriction on K-government, in the sense of Kayne (1983), then the agreeing C K-governs α in both English and French, in that it precedes it, but I does not. On the other hand, the same result can be produced by a c-command restriction on K-government, where it is crucial that the relation be c-command as defined by Reinhart (1976), rather than m-command in the sense of Chomsky (1986a). Indeed, I m-commands α in (43), but it does not c-command it, whereas C both c-commands and m-commands α. The two notions of K-government that distinguish between I and C in (43) can be referred to as the *linear* definition and the *hierarchical* definition, respectively, following Rizzi's (1990) usage. (60) is based on the hierarchical definition, which Rizzi's empirical evidence indeed favors.

(60) β K-governs α iff β is a head, β Case-marks α, and β c-commands α.

Under (60), then, agreeing C K-governs α in (43), because it c-commands it, but I does not, as desired.

Under (60), as before, if α must be K-governed by C, then C must be in the agreeing form, *qui* in French and zero in English, explaining *that-t* and *que-qui* effects. However, contrary to Rizzi's (1990) theory, which contains an explicit head government requirement, nothing in the theory proposed here so far forces any element to be θ-governed, or indeed K-governed, K-government now succeeding θ-government in the statement of the ECP, as in (61). (61) simply states that a non-K-governed element is subject to more stringent requirements than a K-governed element (namely, antecedent government); but as long as antecedent government is satisfied, nothing forces K-government to hold.

(61) *ECP*
   If α is a trace, there is an antecedent β for α such that
   a. α is K-governed and there is a c-set $(\beta, \ldots, \alpha)$ that satisfies government; or
   b. (β, α) satisfies government.

It is at this point that the theory I am proposing parts company with Rizzi's (1990) theory, no less than with Chomsky's (1986a). Under Rizzi's (1990) ECP, which explicitly requires head government, *that-t* effects are automatically derived. What I will maintain instead is that K-government simply discriminates between elements that undergo antecedent government and those that do not, as in (61). I will then show that the *That-t* Filter follows nonetheless, as does the *Wh-t* Filter.

Suppose first that agreement of I and C does not take place in (43). If so, neither I nor C K-governs α; hence, α must move to the Spec of CP position in order to satisfy antecedent government. This straightforwardly derives *wh-t* effects. In turn, if α moves to the Spec of CP position, then α not only agrees with I, but is also coindexed with its antecedent in the Spec of CP. If Spec-head agreement holds between the Spec of CP and C, then α agrees with C as well, and the two heads I and C ultimately agree with one another, because they both agree with α. This means that the *que-qui* agreement rule must apply in French and C must be zero in English, yielding *that-t* effects.

Suppose on the other hand that agreement of I and C does take place in (43), so that α is K-governed by C. Then *that-t* effects follow straightforwardly from the fact that C agrees with I and thus must be in the agreeing form, *qui* in French and zero in English. As for the *Wh-t* Filter, it follows from the fact that if the Spec of CP agrees with C and C agrees with I, then the Spec of CP agrees with I; hence, the Spec of CP cannot contain anything but an antecedent for α. Finally, the fact that subjects display no (long-distance) antecedent government effects is also correctly predicted. For if C agrees with I, and hence the subject is K-governed by C, the subject can simply satisfy government via a c-set.

Strictly speaking, the preceding account is not sufficient to predict the *que-qui* alternation in French. Indeed, it is valid only if agreement of C and I can take place independently of subject movement. This is compatible with the fact that the agreeing form of C, the zero morpheme, can appear independently of subject movement in English. But the *que-qui* alternation in French does depend on the fact that the subject moves. In order to predict the French data, some additional stipulation will then be needed. Suppose for instance that agreement of C and I can be triggered only in case C or its Spec belongs to a *wh*-dependency. In this case it is actually necessary for the subject to move, in order for the agreement of C and I to be triggered, as desired.

To sum up this account of the *That-t* and *Wh-t* Filters: A subject in the Spec of IP position, such as α in (43), is not K-governed by I, but it is K-governed by C if agreement of C with I takes place. Suppose that agreement does not take place. The subject is then forced to move through the Spec of CP position, whence the *wh-t* effects; furthermore, as a consequence of the agreement of their Specs, the C and I heads are in fact forced to agree, whence the *that-t* effects. Suppose on the other hand that agreement does take place; then the *that-t* effects automatically follow. As for the *wh-t* effects, they also follow because the Specs of the agreeing C and I heads cannot disagree. What is more, the subject is K- governed; hence, it can move in one step, accounting for the acceptability of *wh*-island violations of the type in (46).

Finally, as Rizzi (1990) points out, agreement of C and I is only one of the devices that can be used to make a subject extractable under head government, or in present terms K-governed and extractable independently of antecedent government. Another such device is the resumptive pronoun strategy that some languages employ. A third is found in languages like Italian, and in general all null subject languages in the sense of Rizzi (1982). In these languages extraction of the subject can simply take place from a position other than the Spec of IP position—namely, a postverbal position that is to be identified, according to Rizzi (1982) and Burzio (1986), with the VP-adjoined position α in (62). As shown in (63), which translates English (28), there are no *that-t* effects in Italian; and as shown in (64), which translates (25), there are no *wh-t* effects either.

(62)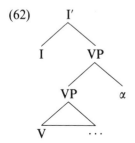

(63) Chi$_i$ pensi [che sia un pittore t$_i$]

(64) Chi$_i$ non sai [cosa$_j$ abbia dipinto t$_j$ t$_i$]

Under the definition of K-government in (60), an inverted subject in Italian in the position of α in (62) is indeed K-governed by I, which Case-marks and c-commands it. Thus, the theory correctly predicts that no agreement mechanisms between C and I are required in Italian.

2.5 Unification of Antecedent Government and Head Government

So far, section 2.1 was largely devoted to subject, adjunct, and complex NP islands, as accounted for by Subjacency, section 2.2 to *wh*-islands, as accounted for by antecedent government, and section 2.4 to the *That-t* Filter, as accounted for under head government. Section 2.3 represented the first attempt here at formulating a unified theory of locality, one that reduces the double disjunction between Subjacency and the ECP, and between θ-government (or K-government) and antecedent government within the ECP, to a single disjunction. Unfortunately, the disjunction between non-K-governed elements, which must satisfy antecedent government, and K-governed elements, which can satisfy government via a c-set, still survives, as in (39) or (61).

Let us concentrate on the nonstandard half of this disjunction, according to which a K-governed trace can satisfy government via a c-set, that is, any random collection of positions ordered by c-command that connects it with an antecedent. Suppose we replace c-sets by some construct based not only on c-command but also, like the notion of chain, on coindexing: specifically, the notion of *sequence*, as in (65), which overlaps with the notion of chain not only in the c-command requirement, but also in the requirement that only positions with the same index are included.

(65) $(\alpha_1, \ldots, \alpha_n)$ is a sequence iff for all α_i, α_i c-commands and is
       coindexed with α_{i+1}.

Crucially, let us assume that there are two types of index in the grammar. The first, which we may call a *categorial* index, is associated with lexical, or categorial, content and can be defined simply as an index associated with every categorial head projected from the lexicon to the syntax, as in (66).

(66) An index *i* is licensed as the categorial index of α iff α is lexical.

Categorial indices are intended to provide a reconstruction of the standard notion of referential index within the theory I am proposing. In the case of N heads, they subsume referential indices; in the case of other lexical heads, such as V, they are meant to eliminate any confusion inherent in the term *referential*.

More significantly, let us assume that a second type of index is defined in the grammar. This is a positional index, associated with some but not all positions; borrowing from Vergnaud (1985), we may call indices of this type *addresses*. The idea is that addresses are associated with K-governed positions. As for their origin, essentially two possibilities arise. One possibility is that every time a K-government relation is established, some ad hoc index is assigned to the K-governed element. Another, more restrictive possibility is that there is fundamentally only one type of index in grammar, the categorial index. Certain categorial indices then become addresses in case K-government holds.

There are in turn two ways to think about addresses as being derived from categorial indices. Under K-government by a head, the categorial index associated with the K-governed element can become lodged at the K-governing head, as in (67). Alternatively, under K-government, the categorial index of the K-governor can become lodged at the K-governee, as in (68). In what follows we will adopt the latter conception.

(67)
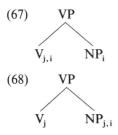

(68)

To be more precise, let us assume that an address is an ordered pair of categorial indices (j, i), associated with α of categorial index i just in case β of categorial index j K-governs it. This corresponds to representations of the type in (69) and to the notion of address in (70). In short, the grammar now includes two types of indices, categorial indices, as in (66), and addresses, as in (70).

(69)
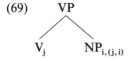

(70) A pair of indices (j, i) is licensed as the address of α iff there is a $\beta = \beta_j$ that K-governs $\alpha = \alpha_i$.

Given this formalism, sequences as defined in (65) can be formed both on the basis of a shared categorial index and on the basis of a shared address. Under (65)–(66), chains correspond to categorial index sequences. Indeed, a number of properties of chains reduce to properties of categorial coindexing. In particular, under the assumption that two categorially coindexed elements share all of their lexical content, no more than one lexical element can be included in each sequence, or chain. All other elements included in the sequence must be empty categories, or else copies of some sort. Similarly, a phrasal lexical element must be matched in the sequence by phrasal empty categories, a head by heads, and so on.

The interesting question is what happens if an address, rather than a categorial index, is taken as the basis for sequence formation. In previous examples in which government was satisfied in a sequence that was not a chain, Vs and their related functional heads were used to connect a trace and an antecedent. We will indeed assume that the properties of addressing force address-based sequences to take this form.

Suppose that indices in general, and hence addresses in particular, can percolate upward as long as they do not encounter incompatible indices. Consider then an addressing configuration of the type in (69). NP is assigned the address (j, i), but the V projection that immediately dominates it is not assigned any address. We can then assume that the address of NP can percolate up to VP. By the same reasoning, it can percolate up to IP, to CP, and so on. The V, I, and C heads of VP, IP, and CP, respectively, can then bear the address (j, i), since they share this property with their maximal projections. Because sequences include a c-command requirement, it will be these heads, V, I, and C, that enter address-based sequences, and not their maximal projections.

Notice that percolation of categorial indices is blocked in all cases, by the intervention of a new (lexical) head above each phrasal constituent. Thus, standard coindexing (with an empty position) is forced to take place, if a categorial index sequence is to be formed. By contrast, the proposed coaddressing mechanism has less in common with coindexing than with notions ranging from Kayne's (1981a, 1983) g-projections and Pesetsky's (1982) paths to Gazdar et al.'s (1985) percolation conventions.

The proposed theory of indexing can now be used to eliminate the residual disjunction within the ECP. The relevant principle, to be called simply *Locality*, is formulated as in (71).

(71) *Locality*

If α is a trace, there is an antecedent β for α and a sequence $(\beta, \ldots, \alpha)$ that satisfies government.

If a trace α is not K-governed, it can have a categorial index but not an address; hence, it can form only categorial index sequences, or chains, not addressed-based sequences. If so, the government requirement in (71) reduces to an antecedent government requirement, as desired. On the other hand, if α is K-governed, it has an address. Hence, α can form an address-based sequence including, in addition to it, any number of heads with which it is coaddressed. In this case, we will see that the government requirement in (71) has the force of Subjacency.

Remember that given the definition of barrier in (23), government subsumes Subjacency not only when applied to chains, but also when applied to c-sets, as in (39). If so, then government subsumes Subjacency when applied to address-based sequences as well, since address-based sequences, like chains, are just a subset of c-sets. In other words, the government requirement in (71) subsumes Subjacency for all traces. What remains to be checked is that (71) subsumes antecedent government, hence in practice predicts *wh*-islands, only for chains, and not for address-based sequences. Consider first the extraction of an adjunct from a *wh*-island, as in (18), repeated here.

(18) *How$_i$ do you wonder [what$_j$ to repair t$_j$ t$_i$]

Since the adjunct is not K-governed, it is not addressed; thus, it can form a categorial index sequence (a chain), but not an address-based sequence. The chain in turn can include traces in IP-adjoined position and VP-adjoined position, as in (72), but not a trace in the Spec of CP position, which is filled by another *wh*-element. Since CP is a barrier for t_i in (72), movement to t'_i across CP obviously violates government, correctly predicting the ungrammaticality of (18).

(72)

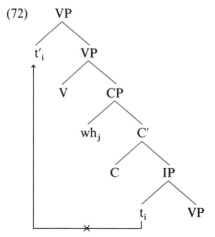

Consider on the other hand the extraction of a direct object from a *wh*-island, as in (15), repeated here.

(15) What$_i$ do you wonder [how$_j$ to repair t$_i$ t$_j$]

Because an object is K-governed, it is addressed. Extraction can then proceed through the formation of an address-based sequence, which can include all of the positions coindexed with the trace in (73).

(73)

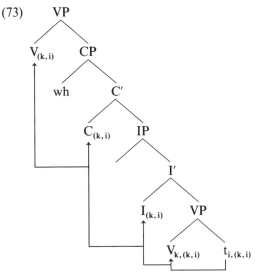

Given this mechanism, the presence of a *wh*-island is irrelevant to the satisfaction of Locality. Crucially, in (73) the matrix V governs the embedded C across the Spec of CP, hence across the *wh*-phrase that fills it; therefore, (15) is correctly predicted to be grammatical with the derivation shown. In general, then, for address-based sequences, and hence for addressed elements, the government requirement in (71) has the force of Subjacency only, as desired.

Before considering further extensions and refinements of the theory, we must take into account a general problem for the unification program in locality that we have been pursuing. Violations of Locality by adjuncts, or in other words violations of antecedent government, typically result in strong ungrammaticality; the intuition is that the constructions in question are uninterpretable. Violations of Locality by objects, or in other words Subjacency violations, typically result in weaker ungrammaticality; the intuition is that the relevant constructions are ill formed but not uninterpretable. In this sense, (4), a pure Subjacency violation, is better than (18), a pure antecedent government violation.

(4)   *What$_i$ does [repairing t$_i$] bother you

(18) *How$_i$ do you wonder [what$_j$ to repair t$_j$ t$_i$]

The question is whether the reduction of antecedent government and Subjacency to a single government principle, as in (71), still allows us to capture this contrast.

It is useful in this respect to again compare the theory proposed here to Rizzi's (1990) theory. In Rizzi's theory only arguments have an index; hence, only arguments can form a dependency by binding. If Subjacency is violated in the process, this violation does not lead to uninterpretability. Since adjuncts do not have an index, they can form a dependency only by forming a chain. If government is violated, chain formation is blocked; hence, the resulting violation leads to uninterpretability, because no dependency has been established at all. Thus, the contrast between the two types of violation is indeed derived.

In one respect, the theory proposed here is essentially like Chomsky's (1986a) theory, since the movement of an index is the only way to establish antecedenthood. However, the distinction between Subjacency and antecedent government also corresponds in the theory proposed here to a principled distinction, between addressed and unaddressed positions. Notice then that an addressed empty category, independently of its link to an antecedent, bears a relation to a head. By contrast, a nonaddressed empty category only bears a relation to an antecedent. Thus, when Locality is violated in an address-based sequence it is still possible to recover the original movement site, whereas there is no independent way to recover it when Locality is violated in a categorial index dependency. Therefore, we can expect the latter situation, but not the former, to produce uninterpretability, as desired.

2.6   Subjects and PPs

Let us reconsider the behavior of subjects under extraction. In the preceding discussion, subject extraction motivated the definition of K-government in (60), as Case marking and strict c-command by a head. This is of course the notion of K-government now built into the definition of address, as in (70). But in what follows we will see that the theory I am proposing allows the notion of K-government to be simplified. The basic use of c-command within the theory is as an ordering relation in the definition of sequence. Now, suppose we require that an address-based sequence must contain not only an addressed element but also its addressing head. If so, it is not necessary to stipulate that the addressing head must c-command the addressing element, since this simply follows from the c-command requirement on sequences. Thus, the notion of K-government can be simplified back to that of Case marking by a head, as in (59).

Remember that we have defined an address (j, i) to be licensed on α just in case α has categorial index i and there is a β with categorial index j such that β K-governs α. In order to force a sequence to include both an addressed element and its addressing head, we can then simply require that every index must be licensed in a sequence, as in the revised definition of sequence in (74).

(74) $(\alpha_1, \ldots, \alpha_n)$ is a sequence iff for all i α_i c-commands and is
       coindexed with α_{i+1}, and every index is licensed in the sequence.

In fact, the additional requirement in (74) can apply to indices in general; since categorial indices are nonrelational, they can trivially satisfy it. Intuitively, exactly as a categorial index uniquely identifies a given category by its lexical content, so an address uniquely identifies a position by the categorial index of a phrase that occupies it, paired with the categorial index of a head that is in a K-government configuration with it. What (74) expresses is simply the requirement that this identification take place sequence-internally.

Consider again the crucial instances of subject extraction, as in (24), (25), and (28), in the light of (74).

(24)   Who$_i$ do you believe [t$_i$ is a painter]

(25)   *Who$_i$ do you wonder [what$_j$ t$_i$ painted t$_j$]

(28)   *Who$_i$ do you believe [that t$_i$ is a painter]

Suppose first that extraction takes place via chain formation. Government can of course be satisfied only if the next landing site for the subject is the Spec of CP, as indicated in (75).

(75)

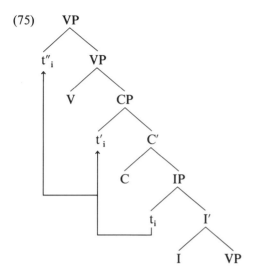

This then forces the Spec of CP position to be empty, whence the *wh-t* effect in (25). Furthermore, agreement between C and the subject in the Spec of CP position induces agreement between C and the Spec if IP position and therefore ultimately between C and I, whence the *that-t* effect in (24) versus (28), on the assumption that the agreeing form of C is zero in English.

Consider next extraction via address-based sequences. Suppose first that we take I to K-govern the subject under (59) and hence to address it. Under (74), every address-based sequence that includes the subject must include I as well; but this is impossible because of the c-command require-ment in (74), since I does not c-command the subject. Hence, the forma-tion of an address-based sequence is blocked. Suppose then that I agrees with C, so that we can take C to K-govern and address the subject. All requirements in (74) can now be satisfied in an address-based sequence, as indicated in (76).

(76)   VP

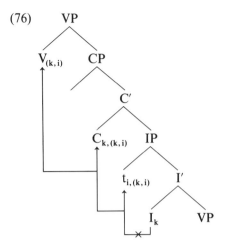

Since C and I agree, however, the *that-t* effect in (24) versus (28) is predicted to arise, under the assumption that the agreeing form of C is zero in English. Similarly, the *wh-t* effect in (25) follows, on the assumption that agreement between I and C implies agreement between their Specs, and hence once again the inability of the Spec of CP to be filled by some other *wh*-phrase.

Thus, the definition of K-government, no longer needs to contain a c-command requirement, since this requirement now follows from the requirement in (74) that indices must be licensed in a sequence. Although this development in the theory does not lead to any empirical gain, it does lead to an important conceptual clarification, in that the one role of c-command in the theory proposed here remains that of ordering sequences and of ordering address relations only within sequences. Indeed, to the extent that only this theory can yield such a result, it thereby gains conceptual support.

Consider next extraction of a PP, or of an argument of P. If the PP is in object position, there is no doubt that it behaves like an argument under extraction from *wh*-islands, as in (77), or that the object of P does likewise under P-stranding, as in (78).

(77) [To which students]$_i$ do you wonder [how$_j$ to speak t$_i$ t$_j$]

(78) [Which students]$_i$ do you wonder [how$_j$ to talk to t$_i$ t$_j$]

Consider first the P-stranding case, as in (78). One obvious way to derive the well-formedness of (78) is to treat V and P as a single discontinuous lexical item, translating into the theory proposed here the idea that (78) instantiates a form of V-P reanalysis. Since lexical content is formalized in this theory by categorial indices, the fact that V and P form a single lexical item can be formalized by assigning them the same categorial index. If this index is furthermore assigned to the object of P under Case marking, then the latter is addressed, and (78) is straightforwardly predicted to be well formed as an instance of address-based extraction, with the partial structure in (79).

(79)

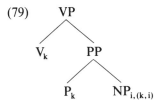

Next let us consider what the structure of PP is, in the absence of V-P reanalysis. Under current accounts, the lexicon is taken to include two major classes of categories: lexical categories, corresponding roughly to open-class items such as N and V, and functional categories, corresponding roughly to closed-class items such as C and I. But as soon as the distinction between lexical and functional categories is introduced within a grammar that includes the theory proposed here, the question arises whether the relevant notion of lexical element for categorial index assignment is "element listed in the lexicon" or "non-functional element." Here we will assume that the latter conception is correct; thus, functional categories are formally distinguished by the fact that they lack a categorial index of their own. Next the question arises whether Ps are lexical or not. Suppose we assume that Ps are nonlexical, and hence not associated with a categorial index. Let us then assume that like addresses, categorial indices are allowed to percolate up a tree until they meet an incompatible index. We then arrive at a structure like (80), where the PP is associated with a categorial index and can of course move by forming a chain.

(80)

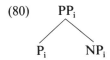

In order to predict the well-formedness of examples like (77), a mechanism for addressing whole PPs appears to be needed. Crucially, in the absence of reanalysis with V, we have effectively treated PP not just as a functional projection, lacking a categorial index of its own, but specifically as a functional projection of NP, to which the categorial index of NP percolates, as in (80). Pursuing this line of thinking, we can assume that V addresses a PP object, exactly as it addresses an NP object, as in (81).

(81)   VP

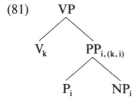

V_k $PP_{i,(k,i)}$

P_i NP_i

Intuitively, in (81) P can be thought of as the realization of the Case of NP. Of course, the well-formedness of (77) as an address-based extraction is predicted on the basis of an indexed structure like (81).

But consider (79) again. Part of the address-based derivation for (77) is that the address of the NP in (79) percolates up to PP, so that a well-formed link of a sequence (P, NP) is created. If so, the question arises whether the address percolated from NP to PP can also be used by PP to form its own address-based sequence. In this particular case, if PP can form a sequence based on the address of NP, this only means that (77) has a well-formed address-based derivation based on (79), as well as one based on (81). However, the same question that we asked about PP can be asked about the VP dominating PP in (79) or indeed (81). In other words, we can ask whether an address percolated from PP to VP can be used by VP to form an address-based dependency; and so on. Thus, a whole set of potential cases of overgeneration can now be seen to arise, where a non-addressed category uses a percolated address to form an address-based dependency. It is obvious that these cases must be excluded.

Now, although the address of NP can and must percolate to PP in (79), under (74) the percolated address cannot be used by PP to form an address-based dependency. This is because under the c-command requirement, if the sequence contains PP, it cannot contain NP; but if the sequence does not contain NP, it does not contain any element of categorial index i, in violation of the licensing requirement. In the case of (79), this now excludes address-based extraction for the whole PP; thus, the only possible derivation for (77) remains the one based on (81). More generally, by exactly the same reasoning that applies to the PP in (81), (74) prohibits the VP in (79) or (81) from forming an address-based dependency using the address percolated from NP; and so on for IP, CP, etc. Indeed, the theory now excludes the entire class of potential overgenerations of this type.

2.7 A-Movement and Head Movement

The unification of locality formalized in (71) is in fact a unification of locality for $\bar{\text{A}}$-movement, in other words, for movement of phrasal constituents to Ā-position. Two other major types of movement have been excluded from the discussion: A-movement (phrasal movement to an A-position) and head movement (movement of a head to another head position). If the theory is correct, it should extend to these other types of movement as well.

First consider A-movement. Chomsky (1981) accounts for A-movement by means of binding theory, and specifically by means of Binding Condition A. Binding theory consists essentially of two conditions, both dependent on the notion of governing category. Binding Condition A requires an anaphor to be bound in its governing category; Binding Condition B requires a pronominal to be free in it. The governing category for an element α is defined in the core cases as the minimal category that dominates α, a governor for α, and an (accessible) subject. A governor for α in the relevant sense is always a head.

The Binding Conditions can easily be restated in a barriers format. First consider Binding Condition A. Instead of saying that an anaphor α must be bound in its governing category γ, we can say that α must be bound by some β such that γ does not exclude β. As for Binding Condition B, instead of saying that a pronominal α cannot be bound in its governing category γ, we can say that α cannot be bound by any β such that γ does not exclude β. Binding theory can then be reformulated as in (82).

(82) *Binding Theory*
   A. If α is an anaphor, there is some β such that β binds α and the governing category for α does not exclude β.
   B. If α is a pronominal, there is no β such that β binds α and the governing category for α does not exclude β.

The question that immediately arises is whether the notion of governing category relevant for (82) can be unified with notions of barrier relevant for locality conditions on movement, and specifically with the notion adopted here. Trivially, a barrier and a governing category share the property that they dominate the element α for which they are defined. More significantly, it can be argued that Chomsky's (1981) notion of governor is in fact reconstructed in the theory proposed here by the notion of g-marker. If so, the definition of governing category can be revised, in terms of this theory, to state that β is a governing category for α just in case it dominates α, a g-marker for α, and an (accessible) subject. Then, the major difference between a governing category and a barrier is that the definition of governing category refers to the notion of (accessible) subject, whereas the definition of barrier does not. Indeed the definition of barrier in (23) is essentially a minimality definition, in that it incorporates, via the notion of g-marker, the idea that the maximal projection of a head creates an opacity domain that includes every element c-commanded by the head. But Chomsky's (1986a) notion of minimality barrier is a close relative of the notion of governing category; indeed, the notion of governing category relevant to binding theory can be seen as the precursor of all notions of minimality.

Let us then consider the object α of a sentence. Under the subject-based definition, the governing category for α necessarily contains the subject β of the sentence. Thus, the correct prediction follows that an anaphoric α can always be bound by β. Suppose on the other hand that we eliminate the notion of subject from the definition of governing category, thus unifying it with the definition of barrier in (23). Since VP is a maximal projection that dominates the object α and its g-marker (namely, V), VP is a barrier for α. Hence, given a theory where the subject β is in the Spec of IP position, the incorrect prediction apparently follows that an anaphoric α can never be bound by β under government.

Two types of solution have been proposed for this problem. The first, advocated by Sportiche (1988), is that the Spec of IP is a derived subject position. The base-generated position for the subject is actually non-VP-external, to be identified with the Spec of VP position, as in Koopman and Sportiche 1990, or with a VP-adjoined position, as in Manzini 1983, 1988. Under this theory, the canonical structure of a sentence is as in (83), where the base-generated subject position is designated by β and the object position by α.

(83)

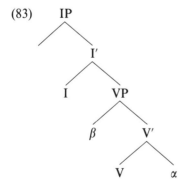

Since in (83) β is not excluded by VP, even if VP is a barrier, it is correctly predicted that an anaphoric α can be bound by β under government, and hence ultimately that an anaphoric α can be bound by the subject in its derived position, the Spec of IP.

The second type of solution is suggested by Chomsky (1986a). It requires no other subject position than the Spec of IP, but it involves the idea that in a canonical sentential structure the heads V and I are systematically related by movement or by some other dependency. In this respect, then, A-movement and head movement crucially interact. Let us take the existence and the properties of the relevant head dependency for granted and simply notate it by coindexing V and I, as in the canonical sentence structure in (84), where β and α again represent the object and subject position, respectively.

(84)

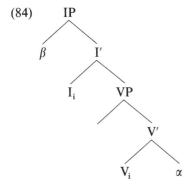

Chomsky's (1986a) idea is that if α moves to β in (84), then the A-chain (β, α) can be extended by the inclusion of the head chain (I, V); indeed, it can be argued that the two chains are coindexed, since I is coindexed with β by Spec-head agreement.

Consider on the other hand the (derived) subject α of a sentence. The relevant configuration is as in (85).

(85)

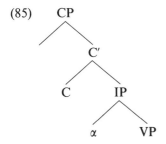

Under definition (23), IP is not a barrier for its Spec α, which is g-marked by C; but CP is, since it dominates α and the g-marker for α, C. Of course, in $\bar{\text{A}}$-movement cases the CP barrier can be circumvented by moving from α to the Spec of CP position. However, there is no position not excluded by CP that can A-bind α, and α is predicted not to be able to A-move from its position in (85), if antecedent government applies to it.

In summary, the discussion so far leads to the conclusion that the notion of governing category in (82) can be identified with the notion of barrier in (23), though only if there is a VP-internal subject or alternatively the locality domain of the object is extended by a systematic dependency between V and I. The former assumption is the one we will adopt here. Of course, if we identify the notions of barrier and of governing category, we can formulate the Binding Conditions in terms of government. This yields the formulation of binding theory in (86), where Binding Condition A turns out to be formally identical to the antecedent government clause of the ECP and hence is subsumed by Locality.

(86) *Binding Theory*
   A. If α is an anaphor, there is an antecedent β for α such that (β, α) satisfies government.
   B. If α is a pronominal, there is no antecedent β for α such that (β, α) satisfies government.

The unification of Binding Condition A with the antecedent government clause of the ECP was already achieved by Aoun (1985), but on the basis of a subject-based definition of locality. Under the Locality account, as indeed under Chomsky's (1986a) account, it is the notion of antecedent government that subsumes Binding Condition A.

Concretely, the binding theory in (86), hence Locality, correctly predicts that in (87) neither the embedded object trace nor the embedded subject trace in the Spec of IP position can be bound by the matrix subject, hence that the construction is ill formed. Furthermore, (86) or equivalently Locality, together with the VP-internal subject hypothesis, correctly predicts the well-formedness of examples like (88), where an object trace is bound from the subject position.

(87) *John$_i$ seems [(t$_i$) was hit t$_i$]

(88) John$_i$ was hit t$_i$

Thus, the question whether the theory proposed here can account for A-movement, as well as for $\bar{\text{A}}$-movement, is answered at least in part positively, in that we have shown that the locality properties of A-movement reduce to antecedent government and hence to Locality. Now, the same is true in Chomsky's (1986a) theory, but the fact that A-movement is subject to antecedent government must be stipulated. Indeed, in the canonical cases of A-movement, as in (88), the A-trace is θ-governed in Chomsky's (1986a) terms, and hence is not required to be antecedent-governed. Within the theory proposed here, by contrast, antecedent government must be satisfied unless an address-based sequence can be formed. As it happens, there is a straightforward reason why an address-based sequence cannot be formed in A-movement cases, namely, that an A-trace is never Case-marked and hence never addressed. Thus, the fact that A-movement must satisfy antecedent government also follows without any need for stipulation.

It is important to emphasize that only a theory of locality that includes a Case-based notion of head government can automatically predict that A-traces behave exactly like adjunct $\bar{\text{A}}$-traces with respect to locality. Any θ-based theory of head government predicts that A-traces pattern with $\bar{\text{A}}$-traces of arguments and can account for the fact that A-traces are subject to antecedent government only by stipulating it. Such a stipulation is needed not only in Chomsky's (1986a) theory but also in Rizzi's (1990). The latter has recourse to the fact that the θ-Criterion, in the sense of Chomsky (1981), must be satisfied by an argument in a chain. A chain is then defined so as to include the requirement that antecedent government be satisfied in it. But this antecedent government requirement on chains is precisely what is derived under the theory I am proposing.

Next let us consider head movement. Important motivation for head movement comes from head-final Germanic languages where the V is sentence-final in embedded sentences but in second position in main sentences. In Den Besten 1983 and much related work it is argued that the underlying position of the V is always sentence-final and that in verb-second configurations V has moved to the C position. The initial phrasal position in verb-second configurations corresponds to the Spec of CP. A similar phenomenon is observed in English in matrix questions, where a *wh*-phrase can be moved into the Spec of CP and subject-auxiliary inversion must take place, as in (89). In a head movement framework, subject-auxiliary inversion corresponds to movement from the I position to the C position, as indicated.

(89) What$_i$ will$_j$ [you t$_j$ [do t$_i$]]

Other motivation for head movement and specifically for movement from V to I comes from Emonds (1978), Pollock (1989a), and Chomsky (1991), among others. The crucial data relate to the position of verbal and sentential modifiers and operators such as adverbs, floating quantifiers, and negation, with respect to verbal heads. Consider adverbs, for instance. An adverb like *completely* in English cannot follow a main verb, as in (90); rather, it must precede the verb, as in (91). On the other hand, it must follow auxiliaries, as in (92), and cannot precede them, as in (93).

(90) *John lost$_i$ completely t$_i$ his mind

(91) John completely lost his mind

(92) John has$_i$ completely t$_i$ lost his mind

(93) *John completely has lost his mind

Suppose then that the base generated position of *completely* is the Spec of VP or a position adjoined to VP. According to Pollock (1989a), if V is a main verb, it remains in place; as a consequence, the adverb is correctly predicted to show up to its left. On the other hand, if V is an auxiliary, it moves to I; the adverb is then predicted to show up to its right. Again according to Pollock (1989a), the base-generated position of auxiliaries can be seen in infinitival sentences. Here, main verbs again must remain in place and cannot move to I, as seen in (94)–(95), where *completely* appears to the left and not to the right of the verb. On the other hand, auxiliaries can either move to I or remain in place, corresponding to the two different positions of the adverb in (96)–(97).

(94) *To lose$_i$ completely t$_i$ one's mind

(95) To completely lose one's mind

(96) To have$_i$ completely t$_i$ lost one's mind

(97) To completely have lost one's mind

Accepting then the existence of head movement, as in (90)–(97) or (89), the question is once again whether it conforms to Locality. The fundamental behavior of head movement is described by the Head Movement Constraint, according to which a head can move only to an immediately superordinate head. The constraint is illustrated by contrasts of the type in (98)–(99). In (98) the higher of two auxiliaries can move from the I to the C position. However, in (99) the lower of the two auxiliaries cannot move from its V position directly to the C position, crossing the I position occupied by the first auxiliary.

(98) Will$_i$ he t$_i$ be doing it

(99) *Be$_i$ [he will t$_i$ doing it]

In terms of the theory proposed here, it is easy to see that (98) is grammatical and (99) ungrammatical because the former satisfies antecedent government and the latter does not. The relevant structure is (84). In (84) VP is not a barrier for its head, V, because I g-marks it. Hence, I governs V, and movement from V to I satisfies antecedent government.

Consider on the other hand movement from V to C, past I. IP is of course a barrier for V in (84), since it dominates it and its g-marker I. Hence, movement from V to C crosses a barrier, IP, and violates government. Thus, under the theory proposed here, as under Chomsky's (1986a) theory, there is no need to stipulate the Head Movement Constraint, which simply follows as a subcase of antecedent government.

The remaining problem is whether the theory predicts that traces of V- or I-movement fall under the antecedent government requirement. θ-based theories such as Chomsky's (1986a) and Rizzi's (1990) are unproblematic in this respect, since V and I are not θ-marked, hence are not θ-governed and referentially indexed, respectively. But the theory proposed here also yields the correct predictions, since neither VP nor IP is Case-marked; thus, neither V nor I is addressed. This means that they cannot form address-based sequences, and hence ultimately that they must satisfy antecedent government.

However, N-movement appears to have exactly the same locality properties as V-movement. Consider for instance cliticization as a case of N-movement. As argued notably by Kayne (1989), strictly local cliticization is possible, as in the French example (100), but long-distance cliticization is not, as in (101).

(100)   Jean le$_i$ veut   [t$_i$]
        John it+wants

(101) *Jean le$_i$ veut   voir   [t$_i$]
        John it+wants to see

Consider then the configuration in (102), where NP is K-governed and hence addressed by V.

(102)

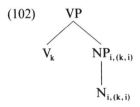

Since we have assumed that addresses percolate from maximal projections to heads, in (102) the address of NP percolates to its head N. If so, we are once more faced with a potential problem for the theory I am proposing, since there is apparently no reason why N in (102) cannot cliticize by forming an address-based sequence; and if this is the case, then long-distance cliticization, as in (101), is incorrectly predicted to be possible.

Now, consider again the requirement in (74) that addresses must be licensed in a sequence. In order to be able to predict that in (102) N, though bearing address (k, i) by percolation, is not able to form a sequence based on this address, we need to explicitly introduce into the theory I am proposing an assumption that has so far been implicit, namely, that Case marking and hence K-government is a relation between a head and a phrase. That a K-governor must be a head is already recognized in the proposed definitions; the assumption that a K-governed element must be phrasal is now introduced in the revised definition of K-government in (103).

(103) β K-governs α iff β Case-marks α, β a head and α phrasal.

Given (103), it is obvious that the N head in (102) cannot form a sequence based on the address (k, i) under (74). Indeed, if the sequence contains NP, as well as N, then the c-command requirement in (74) is violated. But if the sequence does not contain NP, then the address is not licensed in the sequence, and the licensing requirement is violated.

In summary, the theory proposed here correctly predicts that both A-movement and head movement are always subject to antecedent government. For both predictions, we crucially rely on the notion of addressing as Case marking. Thus, A-traces are never addressed because they are never Case-marked; and the same holds of head traces, on the assumption that Case assignment always involves a phrase. In the absence of addressing, then, the net effect of the theory is an antecedent government requirement on both types of traces.

2.8   (Complex) NP Islands

In order to unify locality, I have introduced essentially one new concept, that of addressing. This concept has two features that set it apart from other concepts of head government. The first is that addressing is based entirely on Case, and does not refer to θ-marking. The proposal that Case enters into head government is not new, but both Chomsky's (1986a) definition of θ-government and Rizzi's (1990) definition of referential indices rely on θ-marking, to the exclusion of Case. The second novel aspect of addressing is that it is a form of indexing. In fact, the idea that head government, or θ-government, has the effect of coindexing a trace with a head or a (θ-)feature on a head goes back at least to Stowell (1981). The crucial novelty in the theory proposed here is that an address is taken to function exactly like a categorial index with respect to sequence formation.

It is important to stress that it would be quite possible to maintain that there are two types of indices in the grammar, either of which can be used to form a dependency, while abandoning the idea that one of the two types of indices, addresses, is defined in terms of Case. Similarly, it could be maintained that the notion of Case is relevant for locality without assuming that Case is encoded as a type of indexing, addressing. But the assumption that addressing is based on Case marking by a head has been empirically motivated in the preceding section on the basis of the fact that A-traces of arguments pattern with adjuncts, rather than with Ā-traces of arguments, with respect to extraction. Of course, a θ-based theory predicts, incorrectly, that A-traces and Ā-traces of arguments pattern together. In fact, the point that there is a fundamental disjunction between Case marking and (the antecedent government clause of) the ECP is made as early as Brody 1982. The question that arises now is whether the conception of addressing as a form of indexing is also supported by empirical evidence.

Let us consider complex NP island violations with CPs in the object position of N. Relevant examples are (10) and (32), repeated here, where an object and an adjunct respectively are extracted. The corresponding structure is given in (104).

(10)   *What$_i$ did you see [many attempts to portray t$_i$]]

(32)   *How$_i$ did you see [many attempts [to portray Mary t$_i$]]

(104)

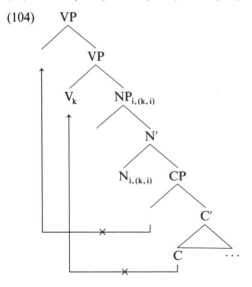

As I will argue, the theory proposed here, and specifically the proposed conception of address-based sequences, allows the ill-formedness both of examples like (10) and of examples like (32) to be derived. Of course, the derivation open to both (10) and (32) via antecedent government is blocked, if we assume that NP does not have an Ā-Spec and that adjunction to NP is blocked by its argument status; for if so, movement can only take place from the Spec of the embedded CP to a matrix VP-adjoined position, crossing the NP barrier, as indicated.

However, consider the alternative derivation open to (10) via an address-based sequence. Let us assume that the sequence has reached the embedded C position. At the descriptive level, all that is needed in order to block movement across NP is the stipulation that N cannot belong to an address-based sequence. However, the theory proposed here provides a principled reason for this. Only a head that does not have an address of its own—that is, whose maximal projection is not Case-marked—can be coaddressed with another element. If it has an address of its own, then coaddressing is impossible, very much as categorial coindexing is impossible between two elements that bear different categorial indices. Now, the NP in (104) is of course Case-marked by V, and hence addressed. N, being itself addressed, cannot be part of a sequence based on a different address; hence, the sequence formed by the object being extracted in (104) must skip N, and government is inevitably violated. This result shows that the theory proposed here differs from other current theories in its range of empirical predictions. In other words, the theory is not simply a notational variant of other current theories, but can be motivated on empirical grounds. Indeed, I know of no other current theory that captures the fact that Ns have a blocking effect on extractions, except by stipulating it, as Kayne's (1981a) and Cinque's (1991) theories do.

One immediate consequence of the derivation of the Complex NP Constraint within the theory I am proposing is that adjuncts generated directly under NP, rather than within some sentence embedded under NP, are also predicted to be unextractable. Indeed, movement across an NP is always blocked by the proposed version of antecedent government, since NP does not have an Ā-Spec, and adjunction to NP is impossible. The prediction appears to be correct, as in (105).

(105) *[For whom]$_i$ did you see [many letters t$_i$]

A more problematic prediction follows when we consider the extraction of an argument of N, as in (106).

(106) Who$_i$ did you see [many pictures of t$_i$]

We can assume that an argument of N is Case-marked and hence addressed by it. Thus, though extraction through the formation of a categorial index sequence is blocked exactly as in the case of adjuncts, an address-based sequence can also be formed. Unfortunately, however, the N that addresses the trace in (106) is itself addressed, hence cannot be used for coaddressing, whereas coaddressing the trace directly with V violates government exactly as in (104). Examples like (106) are then incorrectly predicted to be ill formed.

A possible alternative account of sentences like (106) is that they involve some kind of reanalysis, so that the object of N is extracted only insofar as it has effectively become the object of V. Interestingly enough, the proposed addressing mechanism allows us to capture the idea of reanalysis in these contexts in a natural way. Suppose we assume that given a position Case-marked by a head, that position can be assigned the categorial index of the head that Case-marks it, or, if the Case-marking head is itself addressed, its address. This corresponds to the redefinition of the notion of addressing in (107).

(107) (J, i) is licensed as the address of α iff $\alpha = \alpha_i$ and there is a $\beta = \beta_J$ such that β K-governs α, where $J = j$ (j the categorial index of β) or $J = (k,j)$ ((k,j) the address of β).

Let us consider the structure relevant for (107), namely, (108).

(108)

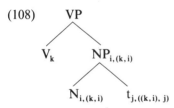

In (108) V Case-marks the higher NP and assigns it address (k, i). Suppose then that the head of NP, N, with categorial index i and address (k, i), itself Case-marks and addresses the lower NP, represented by a trace. Under the hypothesis we are considering, N can assign address (i, j) or address $((k, i), j)$ to the trace. Suppose that the latter is the case, as in (108); the idea is that a well-formed address-based sequence can be formed including the trace, the N head, and the V head in this construction. Technically, in order for this idea to work, it is necessary to assume that sequence formation can be based not only on the same index, but also on compatible indices. Thus, we can assume that in (108) it is the address of the higher NP (k, i) that percolates up to VP and beyond. On the other hand the embedded NP-trace, of address $((k, i), j)$, can form an address-based dependency with N, of address (k, i), and with other superordinate heads that get this address by percolation, because the two addresses are compatible.

More formally, indices can be defined to be compatible just in case an inclusion relation holds between them; the definition of sequence can just as easily be revised to provide for well-formed sequences based on index compatibility as opposed to coindexing, as in (109)–(110).

(109) Index i is compatible with index j iff j includes i.

(110) $(\alpha_1, \ldots, \alpha_n)$ is a sequence iff α_i c-commands and has an index compatible with α_{i+1} and every index is licensed in the sequence.

Thus, although the intuitive core of the theory I am proposing is the old idea of reanalysis, the formal problems of reanalysis operations proper— that is, the difficulty of formulating changes in phrase structure independent of movement, and so on—never arise. In general, then, the theory predicts that whereas V and its associated functional categories act as bridges for extraction, N has the effect of blocking it. To the extent that N can be crossed at all, reanalysis must have applied in the sense just defined.

To sum up: As table 2.1 illustrates, the theory proposed here now includes one definition of barrier, as in (22)–(23), and one locality principle, as in (71). The price for this simplification of the grammar vis-à-vis the theories considered in chapter 1 is a complication in the theory of indexing, summarized in table 2.2. If the preceding arguments are correct, the proposed theory of indexing is independently justified on empirical grounds, by extraction phenomena from (complex) NPs, thus clinching the argument for the theory I am proposing. For ease of reference, table 2.3 summarizes the empirical predictions this theory now yields, together with the number of the subsection where each is crucially discussed. If we compare these predictions with the desiderata in table 1.4, we see that the theory still fails to account for a number of them. We will tackle these residual problems in the next chapter.

Table 2.1
Theory of locality

β g-marks α iff β is a head and a. β is a sister to α or b. β is a sister to a category that agrees with α.	$(=(22))$
β is a barrier for α iff β is a maximal projection, β dominates α, and if α is g-marked, β dominates the g-marker of α.	$(=(23))$
If α is a trace, there is an antecedent β for α and a sequence $(\beta,\ldots,\alpha)$ that satisfies government.	$(=(71))$

Table 2.2
Theory of indexing

An index i is licensed as the categorial index of α iff α is lexical.	$(=(66))$
β K-governs α iff β Case-marks α, β a head and α phrasal.	$(=(103))$
(J,i) is licensed as the address of α iff $\alpha = \alpha_i$ and there is a $\beta = \beta_J$ such that β K-governs α, where $J = j$ (j the categorial index of β), or $J = (k,j)$ ((k,j) the address of β).	$(=(109))$
Index i is compatible with index j iff j includes i.	$(=(109))$
$(\alpha_1,\ldots,\alpha_n)$ is a sequence iff α_i c-commands and has an index compatible with α_{i+1} and every index is licensed in the sequence.	$(=(110))$

Table 2.3
Predictions made by the theory proposed in chapter 2

	Categorial index dependency	Address-based dependency
Subject island	* (2.3)	* (2.3)
Adjunct island	* (2.3)	* (2.3)
Relative clause island	* (2.3)	* (2.3)
(Complex) NP island	* (2.8)	* (2.8)
Wh-island	* (2.5)	OK (2.5)
That-t	OK (2.6)/* (2.6)	OK (2.6)

Chapter 3
Extensions

3.1 The Referential/Nonreferential Distinction

Rizzi (1990) presents three crucial pieces of evidence against Chomsky's (1986a) notion of θ-government and in favor of a restrictive notion of referential index. First, adverbs that obligatorily cooccur with certain Vs can be argued to be θ-marked by them, and hence θ-governed; however, under extraction they behave like adjuncts, displaying sensitivity to *wh*-islands, as in (1)–(2). Second, idiom chunk NPs can be argued to be θ-marked by V, and hence θ-governed by it; but they again display an adjunct-like behavior with respect to islands, as in (3)–(4). Third, the same arguments and facts hold of measure phrases, as in (5)–(6).

(1) [How carefully]$_i$ do you believe [he worded the letter t$_i$]

(2) *[How carefully]$_i$ do you wonder [who$_j$ t$_j$ worded the letter t$_i$]

(3) [What headway]$_i$ do you believe [he made t$_i$]

(4) *[What headway]$_i$ do you wonder [who$_j$ t$_j$ made t$_i$]

(5) [How many kilos]$_i$ do you believe [he weighs t$_i$]

(6) *[How many kilos]$_i$ do you wonder [who$_j$ t$_j$ weighs t$_i$]

Under Rizzi's (1990) theory, all that is required to explain the behaviors in (1)–(6) is the assumption that adverbs, idiom chunks, and measure phrases are not assigned a referential θ-role, so that they do not have a referential index. Given this assumption, their movement patterns are correctly predicted to follow those of adjuncts, rather than those of arguments.

Cinque (1991) extends the notion of referential index to cover behaviors similar to those in (5)–(6) observed with a wide range of quantified NPs. In particular, in Italian, whereas an NP introduced by the existential quantifier *qualche* 'some' can be extracted across a *wh*-island, as in (7)–(8), an NP introduced by the distributive universal quantifier *ogni* 'every' cannot, as in (9)–(10).

(7)   [QUALCHE RAGAZZA]$_i$, dice   [che trovarà t$_i$]
      some   girl   he says that he will find

(8)   [QUALCHE RAGAZZA]$_i$, non so   [come$_j$ trovarà t$_i$ t$_j$]
      some   girl,   I wonder how   he will find

(9)   [OGNI DICHIARAZIONE]$_i$, dice   [di aver ritrattato t$_i$]
      every statement,   he says   he has retracted

(10) *[OGNI DICHIARAZIONE]$_i$, mi chiedo [perchè$_j$
      every statement,   I wonder   why
      abbia ritrattato t$_i$ t$_j$]
      he has retracted

In Rizzi's (1990) terms, the contrast between (8) and (10) follows if the quantified NP has a referential index in (7)–(8) but not in (9)–(10). However, both of the embedded verbs in (7)–(8) and (9)–(10) assign referential θ-roles; hence, both the *qualche* phrase and the *ogni* phrase are predicted to have a referential index. Thus, although referential θ-role assignment can remain a necessary condition on the licensing of referential indices, another necessary condition appears to be that referential indices are licensed only on phrases that have referential content of some sort. In Cinque's (1991) terms, the difference between (8) and (10) indeed is that the *qualche* phrase in (7)–(8) is referential, whereas the *ogni* phrase in (9)–(10) is nonreferential.

Similarly, according to Cinque (1991), the distinction between D-linked and non-D-linked *wh*-phrases introduced by Pesetsky (1987) can also be subsumed by the referential/nonreferential distinction. Thus, extraction of a D-linked *wh*-phrase produces well-formed results independently of the presence or absence of a *wh*-island, as in (11)–(12). But extraction of a non-D-linked *wh*-phrase depends on the absence of a *wh*-island, as seen in the contrast between (13) and (14).

(11) [Che articoli]$_i$ pensi   [che   abbia letto t$_i$]
      what articles do you believe believe (that) s/he read

(12) [Che articoli]$_i$ non sai   [chi$_j$ t$_j$ abbia letto t$_i$]
      what articles do you wonder who   read

(13) [Che diavolo]$_i$ pensi   [che   abbia letto t$_i$]
      what the hell do you think (that) s/he read

(14) *[Che diavolo]$_i$ non sai   [chi$_j$ t$_j$ abbia letto t$_i$]
      what the hell do you wonder who   read

Cinque (1991) also shows that Italian expressions such as *qualcuno* 'someone' either are associated with a resumptive clitic under clitic left dislocation, as in (15), a behavior they share with other quantified NPs; or else are not associated with a resumptive clitic, but directly bind a variable, as in (16).

(15) Qualcuno$_i$ penso [che   lo$_i$ troveremo t$_i$]
      someone I think (that) we will find (him)

(16) Qualcuno$_i$ penso [che   troveremo t$_i$]
      someone I think (that) we will find

When construed as in (15), *qualcuno* is not sensitive to *wh*-islands, though it is when construed as in (16), as shown by the contrast between (17) and (18).

(17) Qualcuno$_i$ mi chiedo [chi$_j$ t$_j$ lo$_i$ troverà t$_i$]
      someone I wonder who   will find (him)

(18) *Qualcuno$_i$ mi chiedo [chi$_j$ t$_j$ troverà t$_i$]
      someone I wonder who   will find

In order to capture this behavior, Cinque (1991) assumes that *qualcuno* and the like can be used referentially or nonreferentially; if used nonreferentially, *qualcuno* behaves like an operator and binds a variable, as in (15), but it also lacks a referential index and hence is sensitive to *wh*-islands, as in (18).

Finally, Cinque (1991) considers scope reconstruction phenomena, of the type in (19)–(20), pointed out by Longobardi (1990).

(19) [Quanti pazienti]$_i$ pensi   [che ogni medico visiti t$_i$]
      how many patients do you think that that every doctor visits

(20) [Quanti pazienti]$_i$ ti chiedi   [come$_j$ ogni medico visiti t$_i$ t$_j$]
      how many patients do you wonder how   every doctor visits

In (19) the *wh*-phrase can be interpreted as having narrow scope with respect to the embedded quantifier; in (20), however, which differs from (19) only with respect to the presence of a *wh*-island, the narrow scope reading of the *wh*-phrase is impossible. In order to explain these facts, Cinque (1991) assumes that for the *wh*-phrase to interact with another quantifier, it must be nonreferential, even though it can be referential when it does not interact with another quantifier; in the presence of a *wh*-word, as in (20), only the referential reading remains available, whence the lack of interaction with the embedded quantifier.

All of the data in (1)–(20) raise a potential problem for the theory proposed here (henceforth *Locality theory*), most clearly the data in (7)–(20), which motivate the notion of referentiality proposed by Cinque (1991). Indeed, all of the phrases moved in (7)–(20) are clearly K-governed and addressed, so that the notion of addressing appears to be unable to predict any of the relevant contrasts in these examples. However, consider the paradigm in (21)–(24). Sentences like (21), where no *wh*-island is crossed, are perfectly well formed in Italian with extraction of *quanti* 'how many' and stranding of the clitic *ne* 'of them'; but sentences like (22), where *quanti* is moved across a *wh*-island, again leaving behind *ne*, are ill formed. Examples like (23) where *quanti* does not strand the nominal part of its phrase are also well formed; in this case extraction out of a *wh*-island appears to be acceptable, as in (24).

(21) Quanti$_i$ pensi   [che   ne$_k$ visiterà [t$_i$ t$_k$]]
      how many do you think (that) he will visit of them

(22) *Quanti$_i$ ti chiedi   [chi ne$_k$ visiterà [t$_i$ t$_k$]]
      how many do you wonder who will visit of them

(23) [Quanti pazienti]$_i$ pensi   [che   visiterà t$_i$]
      how many patients do you think (that) he will visit

(24) [Quanti pazienti]$_i$ ti chiedi   [chi$_j$ t$_j$ visiterà t$_i$]
      how many patients do you wonder who   will visit

Under Cinque's (1991) theory, it can of course be assumed that *quanti* is not referential and hence does not bear a referential index, thus predicting the ill-formedness of (22). In this case, however, Locality theory also provides a solution. Under our usual assumptions, the phrasal constituent *quanti-ne* is Case-marked and hence addressed by the embedded V. As to the position of *quanti* within this addressed constituent, there are then two possibilities. Under the simple structure for NPs that we have adopted so far, *quanti* can only be a Spec. If so, no address can percolate to it, and it cannot form an address-based dependency, so that the ill-formedness of (22) is automatically accounted for.

Alternatively, let us consider a more complex structure where, following Abney 1987 and many related works, NPs are associated with at least one functional projection, DP, as in (25).

(25)

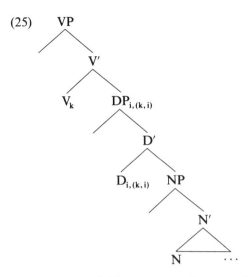

In a structure of this type, *quanti* presumably corresponds to the D head. On the assumption that DP is Case-marked and addressed by V, its address percolates to D, as indicated; hence, *quanti* is in fact addressed. However, we have already established that although heads can be addressed, they can never form address-based sequences. Technically, an address-based sequence is well formed only if the address is licensed within the sequence. Since in (25) the address (k, i) is licensed by the K-government relation between V and DP, both V and DP must be included in a sequence of address (k, i) or the licensing requirement is violated. But DP in turn cannot be included in the sequence with D, since D and DP are not in a c-command relation. Hence, D, or concretely *quanti*, cannot form an address-based sequence, so that Locality theory automatically accounts for the ill-formedness of (22) as an antecedent government violation.

Next let us consider the examples in (23)–(24) more closely. Though they are both well formed, they do not necessarily have the same interpretation. Suppose that the two options available in the syntax are available at LF as well. In other words, either the whole DP or just D can be in operator position, an idea suggested by Dobrovie-Sorin (1990, to appear). If so, there are two LF representations corresponding to examples of the type in (23)–(24). The first, shown in (26)–(27), straightforwardly corresponds to the S-structure configuration. The second, shown in (28)–(29), corresponds to the S-structure configuration in (21)–(22) where the quantifier head has been raised out of its DP.

(26) [How many patients: x] you think that he will visit x

(27) [How many patients: x] you wonder who will visit x

(28) [How many: x] you think that he will visit x patients

(29) [How many: x] you wonder who will visit x patients

In the LF representations in (26)–(27) the DP is Case-marked and addressed by the embedded verb, and a well-formed address-based sequence can be created including both. On the other hand, in (28)–(29) even if D is addressed by the embedded verb, it cannot form an address-based sequence for the same reason as in (21)–(22), namely, that its address cannot be licensed in the sequence. This means in turn that (29) violates antecedent government. Locality theory then predicts that an example of the type in (23) can be associated with the interpretations in both (26) and (28), whereas an example of the type in (24) can be associated only with the interpretation in (27). To the extent that this prediction indeed corresponds to native speakers' intuitions, our hypothesis that the two different LF representations in (26)–(27) and (28)–(29) are in principle possible is confirmed, for the different range of interpretations for (23) and (24) has now been derived from this hypothesis.

With this much background, we can now return to the original problems in (7)–(20). First consider (7)–(10). The contrast between (8) and (10) can now be explained in terms of Locality theory without any recourse to referentiality, if we assume that an *ogni*-type quantifier, as in (10), is compatible only with an LF representation in which D-raising has taken place, and not with one in which where the whole DP is in operator position. Since D cannot form an address-based sequence, it cannot satisfy Locality in the presence of a *wh*-island, and the ungrammaticality of (10) follows. On the other hand, if a *qualche*-type quantifier is compatible with an LF representation in which the whole DP is in operator position, the grammaticality of (8) follows, because the whole DP can form an address-based dependency, insensitive to *wh*-islands. Similarly, consider (11)–(14), and in particular the contrast between the D-linked (12) and the non-D-linked (14). Locality theory must claim that the only interpretation for the non-D-linked *wh*-phrase in (13)–(14) corresponds to an LF representation in which D is in operator position; if so, the impossibility of crossing a *wh*-island, as in (14), is explained. Of course, if the LF representation in which the whole DP is in operator position is also possible for the D-linked *wh*-phrase in (11)–(12), then the theory correctly predicts that no *wh*-island violation will arise, as in (12).

As for (15)–(18), we need not stipulate that the same quantifier can be either referential or nonreferential. Rather, we can simply assume that a quantifier such as *qualcuno* can move either as a head or as a maximal projection. If it moves as a maximal projection DP, it will be able to cross *wh*-islands through the formation of an address-based dependency, as in (17). If it moves as a head D, it will not be able to form an address-based dependency and hence to cross *wh*-islands, as in (18). Finally, with respect to (19)–(20) we can assume that scope interaction between quantifiers requires an LF representation in which D is in operator position. Since this is possible only in the absence of a *wh*-island, the theory predicts, again correctly, that scope interaction between the two quantifiers will be possible in (19), but not in (20).

The potential problems posed by Rizzi's (1990) selected adverbs, idiom chunks, and measure phrases, as in (1)–(6), remain to be considered. Let us look first at measure phrases, as in (5)–(6). Under Rizzi's (1990) theory, all that is required to explain the behavior of measure phrases is the assumption that such phrases are not assigned a referential θ-role, so that they do not have a referential index. Their movement patterns then follow correctly from antecedent government. By contrast, Locality theory apparently predicts examples such as (6) to be well formed, exactly like examples such as (24). One hypothesis that we can pursue, however, is that (6) is ill formed to the extent that it is not only incompatible with a D-raising LF representation for syntactic reasons (because of the presence of a *wh*-island), but also incompatible with a DP-raising LF representation for semantic reasons (related to the difference between *kilos* and *patients*). Indeed, a similar explanation is required by Cinque's (1991) conception of referential indices, if this is construed as substituting for Rizzi's (1990) conception, rather than simply adding to it. In Cinque's (1991) terms, it must be the case that *patients* can be referential, but not *kilos*.

Next consider idiom chunks, as in (3)–(4). The fact that the idiom chunk in (4) moves according to the pattern of adjuncts rather than according to the pattern of direct objects follows under Rizzi's (1990) theory if idiom chunks do not have a referential index. Notice however that all of the idiom chunks considered by Rizzi (1990) are of the form verb-bare nominal. Suppose then that in *make headway* we take the DP projection to be missing altogether in *headway*. Suppose furthermore that although a DP can be an argument, in the technical sense of Chomsky (1981), a bare NP never is. If an NP is not an argument, it need not be θ-marked under Chomsky's (1981, 1986b) θ-Criterion; hence, under Chomsky's (1981, 1986b) Visibility Condition it need not be Case-marked either. We also know that only argument (chains) can be θ-marked under the θ-Criterion. If we assume that under Visibility only argument (chains) can be Case-marked, then an NP, as opposed to a DP, must also be Caseless. This means that if an idiom chunk is an NP and not a DP, it is not K-governed and addressed, and hence it must be antecedent-governed. Its sensitivity to *wh*-islands, as in (4), then follows.

Similarly, consider selected adverbs, as in (1)–(2). Rizzi (1990) suggests that selected adverbs must satisfy antecedent government because they are not referentially θ-marked and hence do not have referential indices. However, adverbs are not arguments and hence need not satisfy Visibility and be Case-marked. More strongly, we can assume that if only arguments can be visible, adverbs cannot be, and hence they cannot be Case-marked. If this is correct then adverbs are never K-governed and addressed, and Locality theory straightforwardly predicts that they must satisfy antecedent government. Indeed, though Rizzi (1990) uses selected adverbials and idiom chunks to argue against Chomsky's (1986a) notion of θ-government, it is clear that the argument does not go through. It is sufficient to adopt something like the theory proposed here under which idiom chunks and adverbs are not arguments in Chomsky's (1981) sense, hence are not θ-marked, in order for them not to be θ-governed either, as desired.

Having now reviewed the empirical evidence relevant for Rizzi's (1990) and Cinque's (1991) notion of referential indices, we can consider more general conceptual issues. Because Cinque's (1991) notion of referential content subsumes Rizzi's (1990) notion of referential θ-role and not vice versa, the immediate comparison is between Locality theory and Cinque's (1991) theory. Crucially, the two theories appear to be equivalent in complexity. In particular, our link between antecedent government and lack of K-government is strictly comparable to Cinque's (1991) link between antecedent government and lack of referential indices. As for the option of raising either D or DP, this must be available independently of Locality theory because of examples of the type in (21)–(24). What Locality theory then says is that the two possible interpretations for examples like (23)–(24) correspond to two LF representations like (26)–(27) and (28)–(29). This is strictly comparable to saying that the two interpretations in (23)–(24) correspond to the presence or absence of a referential index. Finally, via the notion of referential index, Cinque (1991) identifies the two relevant interpretations as referential and nonreferential, respectively. We will leave the relevant interpretations undefined, but given Cinque's (1991) lack of independent semantic characterization for referentiality, the matter appears to be purely terminological.

Consider on the other hand the reconstructions of Rizzi's (1990) and Cinque's (1991) theory by Frampton (to appear a, b), Szabolcsi (1991), and Szabolcsi and Zwarts (1990). According to such reconstructions, the class of dependencies that can be successfully formed across a *wh*-island is characterized by the presence of an operator-variable structure with the variable ranging over individuals, or in other words by the presence of an individual variable, in the sense of Heim (1987). Now, Frampton (to appear a) motivates precisely representations of the type in (26)–(27) and (28)–(29) for sentences involving extraction of *how many*, where (26)–(27), with DP-raising, represent the individual variable reading, and (28)–(29), with D-raising, represent the nonindividual reading. Once given (26)–(29), however, it is clear that our discussion goes through as before. Similarly, consider Longobardi's (1990) scope interaction phenomena. According to Frampton (to appear a), what is involved is the inability of an individual variable to be construed with anything but wide scope. If we assume, as before, that a DP variable corresponds to an individual variable reading, then our discussion goes through unchanged. Similarly, Szabolcsi (1991) comments that D-linked readings are always individual readings. But if individual readings correspond to DP variables, then the correlation between D-linking and DP variables holds, as desired. And so on.

In summary, the logic of the discussion is as follows. Given the availability of both DP-raising and D-raising in the syntax, we can assume that the same possibility is open at LF. The resulting LF representations account for individual variable readings, corresponding to DP variables, and nonindividual readings, corresponding to D variables. Under movement, however, a DP can form address-based sequences, whereas a D cannot. This accounts for the fact that individual readings remain available across antecedent government islands, typically *wh*-islands, but nonindividual readings disappear.

We can now return to one last potentially problematic prediction of Locality theory. If K-government and hence addressing is the relevant criterion for extractability from *wh*-islands, then VPs, which are not Case-marked, are predicted not to be extractable from *wh*-islands. However, Chomsky (1986a) notices that extracting a VP across a *wh*-island does not create a violation comparable to that produced by extracting an adjunct in the same context. On the basis of this, he concludes that VPs are θ-governed by I, from which it follows that they need not be antecedent-governed. Under Rizzi's (1990), theory the data similarly require the assumption that VPs have a referential index, enabling them to move long-distance. But to conclude that VP is an argument, as Chomsky (1986a) does, or that it has referential properties, as Rizzi (1990) does, is as questionable as concluding that VP is Case-marked within Locality theory. Thus, at the conceptual level, if not at the level of realization, the extractability of VP across a *wh*-island is a problem for all theories under consideration.

Notice on the other hand that none of the extractions considered by Cinque (1991) in which nonvisible or nonreferential constituents are moved from *wh*-islands, as in (7)–(20), has the same uninterpretable results as extraction of an adjunct. On the contrary, it appears that the contrast between extractability of a VP in the absence of a *wh*-island and extractability of a VP across a *wh*-island, as in (30)–(31), fully repeats contrasts of the type in (7)–(8), and the like. If so, there is no need for any problematic assumption to the effect that VPs are arguments and/or that they are Case-marked. Rather, (31) can be treated as an antecedent government violation.

(30) [MANGIATO LA MELA]$_i$, credo   [che abbia t$_i$]
      eaten the apple,   I believe that she has

(31) *[MANGIATO LA MELA]$_i$, non so   [chi$_j$ t$_j$ abbia t$_i$]
      eaten the apple,   I wonder who has

3.2 Pseudo-Opacity, Inner, and Factive Islands

In a development of the theory independent of the referential/nonreferential distinction, Rizzi (1990) argues in favor of a definition of antecedent government that crucially employs the notion of potential antecedent, in other words, Relativized Minimality. Rizzi cites two types of islands in support of Relativized Minimality: inner islands in the sense of Ross (1984), and pseudo-opacity islands in the sense of Obenauer (1976, 1984). They belong to the same family as *wh*-islands in that adjuncts are sensitive to them, but objects and subjects are not.

Consider pseudo-opacity first. The data, originally noted by Obenauer (1976), are of the type in (32)–(37).

(32) Il a consulté   [beaucoup de livres]
      he has consulted much of books

(33) Il a beaucoup$_i$ consulté [t$_i$ de livres]
      he has much consulted   of books

(34) [Combien de livres]$_i$ a-t-il consulté t$_i$
      how much of books has he consulted

(35) Combien$_i$ a-t-il consulté [t$_i$ de livres]
how much has he consulted of books

(36) [Combien de livres]$_i$ a-t-il beaucoup consulté t$_i$
how much of books has he much consulted

(37) *Combien$_i$ a-t-il beaucoup consulté [t$_i$ de livres]
how much has he much consulted   of books

Both (32) and (33) are well formed in French. In (32) no movement takes place; in (33) the quantifier *beaucoup* 'a lot (of)' moves, stranding the rest of its DP. Similarly, both of the extractions in (34) and (35) are well formed. In (34) the whole DP moves; in (35), as in (33), the quantifier *combien* 'how much (of)', moves stranding the rest of its DP. However, consider the contrast in (36)–(37). (36), where the whole DP moves across the quantificational adverb, is well formed; (37), where only *combien* moves across *beaucoup*, is ill formed.

Locality theory predicts that movement of the D head *combien* out of its DP will give rise to antecedent government effects. Thus, it correctly predicts that movement of *combien* across a *wh*-island in (39) is ill formed, though movement of the whole DP in (38) is well formed.

(38) [Combien de problèmes]$_i$ sais-tu   [comment$_j$ résoudre t$_i$ t$_j$]
how much of problems do you know how to solve

(39) *Combien$_i$ sais-tu   [comment$_j$ résoudre [t$_i$ de problèmes] t$_j$]
how much do you know how to solve   of problems

Unfortunately, however, this theory does not define any island for antecedent government in (37). By contrast, under Rizzi's (1990) theory, if *beaucoup* is in the Spec of VP, it straightforwardly defines a Relativized Minimality island. It then counts as a potential $\bar{\text{A}}$-antecedent for the *wh*-trace, exactly like the *wh*-phrase in the Spec of CP in (39); hence, the ill-formedness of (37), as well as of (39), correctly follows. What is more, Relativized Minimality predicts a contrast between (40) and (41), where an adjunct is extracted, since the extraction crosses *beaucoup* in (41), though not in (40). As in the case of (36)–(37), Locality theory does not predict any contrast between (40) and (41), because it does not define any antecedent government island in (41).

(40) Comment$_i$ a-t-il résolu beaucoup de problèmes t$_i$
how   did he solve much of problems

(41) *Comment$_i$ a-t-il [beaucoup$_j$ résolu [t$_j$ de problèmes] t$_i$]
how   did he much solve   of problems

Next consider inner islands, as in (42)–(43).

(42) *Why$_i$ don't you think [Peter left t$_i$]

(43)   Why$_i$ do you think [John left t$_i$]

(42) differs from (43) only by the presence versus absence of a sentential negation, *not*. (42) is ill formed with the interpretation under which the adjunct is extracted from the embedded sentence, as indicated, though it is well formed with the interpretation, irrelevant here, under which the adjunct is associated with the matrix verb. (43) is well formed under both interpretations. Inner islands in the sense of Ross (1984) are the islands created by the negation in sentences of the type in (42). It is easily demonstrated that no inner island effects arise with objects, as in (44), and with subjects, as in (45).

(44) What$_i$ don't you think [Peter did t$_i$]

(45) Who$_i$ don't you think [t$_i$ left]

Rizzi (1990) assumes that the negation element *not* is generated in an Ā-Spec. This can be taken to be the Spec of VP; alternatively, if a sentential negation defines a NegP projection of its own, as argued by Pollock (1989a) and Kayne (1989), the negation can be taken to fill the Spec position of NegP. The resulting configurations are then of the type in (46), on the assumption that NegP is generated above VP and under IP.

(46)

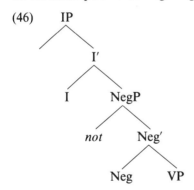

Given structures of this type, the extraction of the adjunct in (42) must at some point cross *not*, a potential antecedent for the adjunct in virtue of its Ā-Spec position. Hence, antecedent government does not hold under Rizzi's (1990) Relativized Minimality, and (42) is correctly predicted to be ill formed. Unfortunately, as before, Locality theory does not define any island in (46) and hence does not predict the ungrammaticality of (42).

Consider again the Locality theory approach to *wh*-islands, the one type of antecedent government islands that the theory derives so far. In the case of *wh*-islands, as in (39), the facts can be accounted for without recourse to Relativized Minimality, by crucially relying on the fact that an adjunct or other unaddressed element can move neither through the Spec of CP, which is already filled by hypothesis, nor through a CP-adjoined position, since adjunction to an argument is impossible. The analogous solution for inner and pseudo-opacity islands is to say that the adjunct not only cannot move through the Spec of NegP or the Spec of VP, for the obvious reason that it is already filled, but also cannot move through a NegP-adjoined or VP-adjoined position.

Suppose we take the radical step of prohibiting adjunction to maximal projections in general. This has the desired consequence of blocking adjunction to NegP and to VP. However, adjunction to VP has previously been assumed to be possible. What, then, are the consequences of our prohibition for VP? Since movement cannot proceed through the VP-adjoined position, there must be a VP-internal escape hatch. This can only be the Spec position, as in the case of CP; but if so, a potential problem arises. Although an infinite number of adjunction sites are available at any given VP, there is just one Spec of VP position. Thus, no two different *wh*-phrases can be extracted through the same Spec of VP, though infinitely many can be extracted through VP-adjoined positions. Now, either a *wh*-phrase can move in one step, in which case it need never use the Spec of VP; or it must move so as to satisfy antecedent government. In the latter case, any two phrases passing through the same Spec of VP have to pass through the same Spec of CP. Hence, movement is blocked at the Spec of CP level in any theory, if not at the VP level as under the hypothesis proposed here. Thus, prohibiting adjunction to VP, and allowing the (unique) Spec of VP to function as an escape hatch appears to be a viable option.

On the other hand, prohibiting adjunction to every maximal projection means prohibiting adjunction to IP as well. Since in this case the Spec position is systematically filled by a subject and cannot be used as an escape hatch by movement, the impossibility of adjunction means that movement must take place directly from the Spec of VP position to the Spec of CP position, crossing the IP barrier. It appears then that adjunction to IP must be allowed, and the strong hypothesis that adjunction is in general impossible cannot be maintained. Let us therefore consider a weaker hypothesis, namely, that adjunction is possible only to those maximal projections that do not have an $\bar{\text{A}}$-Spec. This still prevents adjunction to NegP and VP, while allowing adjunction to IP, as desired.

This hypothesis raises a problem of its own. If it is correct that adjunction and $\bar{\text{A}}$-Specs are in complementary distribution, then the simplest grammar is one in which they are identified. Since CP must have an $\bar{\text{A}}$-Spec, and since we have seen that VP can also have an $\bar{\text{A}}$-Spec, rather than being adjoined to, the question is whether IP also can have an $\bar{\text{A}}$-Spec. One part of the question concerns X-bar theory. For our purposes, it is sufficient to say that for each maximal projection there is at most one $\bar{\text{A}}$-position, whether it is a Spec position or an adjoined one, as in (47).

(47) Each maximal projection is associated with at most one $\bar{\text{A}}$-escape hatch.

The other part of the question concerns the possibility of having a single $\bar{\text{A}}$-position, as opposed to a potentially infinite number of them. The answer to this can be exactly as for VP. Since the presence of a single Spec of CP position limits the number of *wh*-extractions to one per sentence under antecedent government, the availability of one landing site at any other maximal projection does not have any empirical consequences. Thus, the hypothesis that there is at most one $\bar{\text{A}}$-escape hatch per maximal projection, can be maintained. Of course, if adjunction to a maximal projection is now reduced to the single $\bar{\text{A}}$-position in (47), Chomsky's (1986a) requirement that only nonarguments can be adjoined to must be recast as saying that only nonarguments can have an $\bar{\text{A}}$-escape hatch, as in (48).

(48) An $\bar{\text{A}}$-escape hatch can be associated only with a nonargument maximal projection.

Not the least of the advantages of (48) is that it allows CPs to be classed with nonarguments from the point of view of the theory of $\bar{\text{A}}$-positions, as they have been classed, implicitly, for the purposes of the proposed theory of addressing.

The theory of $\bar{\text{A}}$-positions in (47)–(48) is in general very simple and conceptually perspicuous. What it says is that there is at most one operator per maximal projection, as in (47), and that no operator can be associated with arguments. The latter prohibition appears only natural if we think of an argument as an LF variable; in essence, what (48) says is that no variable can be associated with an operator, except of course the operator it is bound by. Though I will not push the matter further, it appears then that (47)–(48) can be subsumed under some general principle that each maximal projection is associated with at most one operator; in the case of a variable, this must be the operator that binds it, whence the prohibition against $\bar{A}$-positions within argument maximal projections. What is immediately relevant here is that under the theory in (47)–(48), pseudo-opacity and inner islands are accounted for straightforwardly on exactly the same grounds as *wh*-islands, as desired. Thus, a quantificational adverb or negation in the $\bar{A}$-Spec of VP or NegP prevents a *wh*-phrase from passing through the same position, exactly as a *wh*-phrase in the $\bar{A}$-Spec of CP does. This forces the crossing of a barrier and hence an antecedent government violation. So far, however, we have limited ourselves to syntactic movement. The question then arises whether there are any cases where multiple adjunctions, as opposed to a single $\bar{A}$-Spec, must be admitted at LF. The obvious candidate is multiple adjunction to IP of quantified expressions, as in LF representations of the type in (49), proposed by May (1985).

(49) [$_{IP}$ Every spy$_i$ [$_{IP}$ some Russian$_j$ [$_{IP}$ t$_i$ suspects t$_j$]]]

May (1985), in fact, following work by Guéron (1981), explicitly suggests that a principle of the type in (47) holds. According to May (1985) multiple adjunction to IP, as in (49), is unnecessary. Thus, he argues that (49) is equivalent to (50), where one quantified DP is adjoined to IP, and the second one is adjoined to the first.

(50) [$_{IP}$ [$_{DP}$ Every spy$_i$ [$_{DP}$ some Russian$_j$]] [$_{IP}$ t$_i$ suspects t$_j$]]

Indeed, in both structures the two operators have the same absolute scope and commute in relative scope. Technically, May (1985) defines a Σ-sequence as in (51), where O stands for an operator.

(51) S is a Σ-sequence iff for all O$_i$ and O$_j$ in S, O$_i$ c-commands O$_j$ and O$_j$ c-commands O$_i$.

May's (1985) Scope Principle then essentially says that members of Σ-sequences are free to take on any type of relative scope relation, as in (52).

(52) *Scope Principle*
If O$_i$ and O$_j$ are members of a Σ-sequence, then O$_i$ and O$_j$ are free in scope with respect to one another.

Notice also that adjunction to DP does not represent a problem for Chomsky's (1986a) theory of adjunctions or the version of it in (48), since by LF the DP that has been adjoined to is no longer an argument but an operator.

Just as two quantifiers adjoined to one another can fill the unique $\bar{A}$-position associated with IP in (50), so two *wh*-phrases that commute in scope are predicted to be adjoined to one another and to cooccur in the same Spec of CP. Since clusters of *wh*-phrases are in fact overtly excluded in English, as in (53), this prediction appears to be incorrect. However, in English multiple *wh*-phrases in the Spec of CP must be admitted at LF in cases of *wh*-in-situ at S-structure. In other words, something like (53) must be the LF representation corresponding to the well-formed (54).

(53) *What$_i$ who$_j$ [t$_j$ saw t$_i$]

(54) Who$_i$ [t$_i$ saw what]

What is more, in Slavic languages multiple *wh*-phrases apparently adjoined to the same site appear at S-structure as well, as discussed for instance by Rudin (1988) or by Brody (1990) for Hungarian. Obviously, some parameter must be responsible for the impossibility of multiple *wh*-phrases at S-structure in English; otherwise, the theory once more makes the correct prediction.

Finally, the preceding discussion only takes into account arguments for Relativized Minimality based on phrasal movement, as presented by Rizzi (1990). However, a number of arguments have recently been published in favor of Relativized Minimality for head movement. Thus, Roberts (1991) suggests that the A/Ā distinction is relevant not only for phrasal movement but also for head movement and that under Relativized Minimality, an A-head is a potential antecedent governor for another A-head, and an Ā-head is a potential antecedent governor for another Ā-head. The crucial empirical evidence includes apparent long head movement patterns of the type in (55) from Portuguese, noted by Lema and Rivero (1990), where a nonfinite form of the verb moves across a clitic + auxiliary complex.

(55) Seguir$_i$- [te-ei   [t$_i$ por toda a parte]]
      follow (I) you-will   everywhere

Such sentences can be analyzed as involving movement of the nonfinite verb to C, across the clitic + auxiliary complex in I. Under this analysis, any version of rigid minimality, including the one adopted here, apparently predicts ungrammaticality, since a head is crossed. By contrast, the revision of Relativized Minimality proposed by Roberts (1991) predicts grammaticality, on the assumption that movement takes place to an Ā-head, C, across an A-head, I.

A detailed examination of the class of data exemplified by (55) is beyond the scope of this book. It will suffice to notice that Lema and Rivero (1990) do not have recourse to Relativized Minimality; the solutions they propose in terms of Chomsky's (1986a) theory are thus perfectly compatible with the present framework.

One open problem remains. This is represented by a type of island that we have not considered so far: factive islands, which involve extraction from the complement of a factive verb. As illustrated in (56) and (57), respectively, adjuncts are sensitive to these islands, but arguments are not.

(56) *Why$_i$ do you regret [that John repaired it t$_i$]

(57) What$_i$ do you regret [that John repaired t$_i$]

This is the same pattern that is found with *wh*-islands and other islands that Rizzi (1990) accounts for via Relativized Minimality. Under this latter theory, as under the version of rigid minimality within which we have reconstructed it here, the facts in (56)–(57) then follow as long as the Spec of the embedded CP can be assumed to be filled by an operator of some sort. The problem is of course that the Spec of CP in (56)–(57) is apparently empty and hence perfectly available for an adjunct to move through.

Indeed, it appears to be a head, the factive verb *to regret*, that creates an island in (56); whereas in all the theories considered so far, adjunct movement is sensitive only to the availability, or unavailability, of Spec positions. A radical alternative to these theories is proposed by Szabolcsi and Zwarts (1990), under which it is indeed *to regret* that renders the extraction of the adjunct impossible in (56). Szabolcsi and Zwarts (1990) observe that the typical contexts in which adjuncts and arguments behave asymmetrically under extraction are contexts that do not preserve entailment. Thus, the simple entailment in (58) is preserved under a verb of the type of *to think*, as in (59), but not under a *wh*-island, as in (60). *To regret*, as in (61), patterns with (60) in that it does not preserve entailment.

(58) John walks quickly → John walks

(59) I think that John walks quickly → I think that John walks

(60) I wonder whether John walks quickly $\not\to$ I wonder whether John walks

(61) I regret that John walks quickly $\not\to$ I regret that John walks

According to Szabolcsi and Zwarts (1990), phenomena of extraction from *wh*-islands reflect, not a syntactic constraint, but a semantic one. Simply, nonindividual variables cannot be bound across configurations that do not preserve implication in the way indicated. Consider, however, a predicate like *to be certain*. This behaves like *to regret* with respect to extraction of adjuncts and arguments, as in (62)–(63); yet it patterns with *to think* in preserving entailment, as in (64).

(62) *Why$_i$ are you certain [that John repaired it t$_i$]

(63) What$_i$ are you certain [that John repaired t$_i$]

(64) I am certain that John walks quickly → I am certain that John walks

Thus, the semantic generalization that Szabolcsi and Zwarts (1990) propose appears to be at best partially successful, and the argument against the type of theory that we are adopting indecisive.

Let us then return to Locality theory, or more generally to theories of adjunct extraction based on antecedent government. Suppose that the Spec of the embedded CP in (56)–(57) is taken to be filled by an empty operator. It appears that the main semantic property of the CP complements of factive verbs is that they denote an individual event. There is therefore semantic motivation for postulating an empty operator, which takes scope over the event that the factive complement denotes, essentially as proposed by Melvold (1986). Syntactically, Hegarty (1990) points out that subject extraction from factive islands appears to be essentially well formed, up to the well formedness of *that* deletion in factive configurations, as in (65).

(65) Who$_i$ do you regret [t$_i$ is a painter]

But subject extraction from a *wh*-island is of course impossible when the subject trace is adjacent to a *wh*-operator.

Now, remember that in Locality theory there are no *wh*-island violations with subjects, but only violations of a local constraint against *wh-t* configurations. Our explanation for this, following Rizzi (1990), is that a *wh*-phrase in the Spec of CP agrees with C, thus preventing the subject from agreeing with C; hence, both escape hatches that are in principle open to the subject are blocked, the Spec of CP by the *wh*-phrase, and C by the fact that it agrees with the *wh*-phrase, making it unavailable for agreement with I and hence for the role of K-governor of the subject. However, there is more than one respect in which the operator that we have postulated in factive configurations differs from a *wh*-phrase. In particular, it appears to be the *wh*-feature that triggers agreement between the head and Spec of CP in English as in other languages. Suppose then that other (empty) operators do not trigger such agreement; in that event, they leave an escape hatch automatically empty for subjects. This effectively disposes of the potential problem for associating operator structures with factive configurations represented by the (relative) well-formedness of (65).

3.3 Wh-Islands and Tense Islands

Let us now consider *wh*-islands again. Locality theory, like Chomsky's (1986a) theory or Rizzi's (1990), predicts that arguments can be extracted from *wh*-islands, but adjuncts cannot. In Locality theory, of course, this is because arguments are addressed, but adjuncts are not. However, if Chomsky (1986a) is correct, although extracting an argument from an untensed *wh*-island does not produce a violation, as in (66), extracting an argument from a tensed *wh*-island does, as in (67).

(66) What$_i$ do you wonder [how$_j$ to repair t$_i$ t$_j$]

(67) *What$_i$ do you wonder [how$_j$ John repaired t$_i$ t$_j$]

Unfortunately, Chomsky's (1986a) solution to the problem in (67) is essentially ad hoc, since it depends on the assumption that a tensed IP exceptionally is an inherent barrier. In turn, this basically reproduces Rizzi's (1982) idea that *wh*-island violations depend on the fact that *wh*-extractions are sensitive to both S and S' nodes.

The theory that we have developed so far also apparently predicts that (66) and (67) are equally well formed. However, it differs from the other theories under consideration in one fundamental respect, which we exploited earlier in deriving (complex) NP islands: namely, that addresses as well as categorial indices can serve as the basis for sequence formation. If a categorial index sequence is formed, then a Locality violation can arise because of the unavailability of local landing sites. Similarly, if an address-based sequence is formed, a Locality violation can arise because no unaddressed heads are available for the sequence to pass through. Thus, in deriving complex NP island violations, we have made crucial use of the fact that an N head generally is addressed. This means that the address-based strategy of extraction is blocked across NP, exactly as the categorial index strategy is blocked by the absence in NP of an Ā-escape hatch.

Now, what appears to be involved in the contrast between (66) and (67) is a ±Tns property of some head. Let us assume for concreteness that this Tense property is realized at a head T. This can be conceived of as one of the functional categories obtained from breaking I into its component parts, as in Pollock 1989a, Chomsky 1991, and related literature. We can then try to derive the contrast between (66) and (67) from Locality theory under the assumption that a +Tns head bears an address, whereas a −Tns head does not. Consider the abstract structure in (68), where a wh-phrase has been moved through the Spec of TP position, leaving a trace t, on its way to some Spec of CP. The presence of the trace effectively creates a wh-island configuration, since we are now working with a theory where there is at most one Ā-escape hatch per maximal projection.

(68)   TP

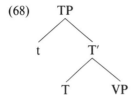

Suppose next that an addressed wh-phrase, such as the argument in (66)–(67), attempts to cross TP through the formation of an address-based sequence. If T is unaddressed, as we assume it is in (66), then the address of an argument wh-phrase can move through it, producing a well-formed extraction. If T is addressed, as we tentatively assume it is in (67), then it is impossible to move an address through it, and a Locality violation results. Thus, the assumption that a +Tns head is addressed, but a −Tns head is not, allows us to predict the contrast between (66) and (67) within Locality theory, without having recourse to any additional stipulations. What is more, the abstract mechanism underlying Tense effects as in (67) is seen to be exactly the same as the mechanism underlying complex NP island violations, as first suggested to me by T. Hoekstra. This means that two otherwise mysterious phenomena receive not only an explanation, but a related explanation.

One immediate problem is that although complex NP islands are, as far as I know, universal, contrasts of the type in (66)–(67) apparently are language-specific, since their Italian counterparts in (69)–(70) are both well formed.

(69) [Che cosa]$_i$ ti chiedi [come$_j$ riparare t$_i$ t$_j$]

(70) [Che cosa]$_i$ ti chiedi [come$_j$ Gianni abbia riparato t$_i$ t$_j$]

This means that Locality theory apparently needs not only some assumption to the effect that a +Tns head is addressed in English, but also some parametric proviso to the effect that a +Tns head is not addressed in Italian. However, an alternative solution that allows us to maintain that a +Tns head is addressed universally can be based on the fact that Italian typically translates the embedded tensed sentence of English in examples like (67) with a subjunctive, as in (70). If subjunctive forms are finite, but untensed, as suggested by Picallo (1984), then the well-formedness of (70), on a par with both (66) and (69), once again follows without need for stipulation.

The most important problem we are left with at this point is the theoretical problem of deriving the assumption that +Tns implies addressing. So far we have assumed that Case Marking by a head implies coindexing with the head, hence addressing. Apparently, however, nothing forces +Tns to be Case-marked (by a head), and hence nothing forces it to be addressed. Suppose we assume that the denotational properties of +Tns mean that it functions essentially as an argument, an idea developed by Guéron and Hoekstra (to appear). As such, we can assume that it is assigned an argument role, perhaps an event role in the sense of Higginbotham (1985). Hence, if the θ-Criterion extends to all argument-type relations, and not only to θ-relations in the sense of Chomsky (1981), then +Tns straightforwardly satisfies it. Furthermore, again following Chomsky (1981), +Tns will be subject to the visibility requirement. If this in turn implies Case-marking +Tns (by a head), then +Tns will also be systematically addressed, as desired under Locality theory.

Thus, it is not difficult to derive from the denotational properties of +Tns the need for it to be visible. The problem is whether visibility means Case marking by a head in this instance, and hence ultimately addressing. Let us consider a generalized conception of addressing, under which Case marking by a head—or, in other words, K-government—is not a necessary condition for the licensing of an address; rather, a visibility relation (to a head) is, as in (71).

(71) (J, i) is licensed as the address of α iff $\alpha = \alpha_i$ and there is a $\beta = \beta_J$ such that α is made visible by β, where $J = j$ (j the categorial index of β) or $J = (k, j)$ $((k, j)$ the address of β).

(72)

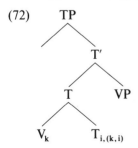

We of course still assume that K-government is a visibility relation, and hence sufficient to satisfy (71); however, (71) is also satisfied by any other visibility relation defined by the grammar. Intuitively, the idea is, as proposed by Baker (1988), that arguments can be licensed with respect to visibility in two ways: phrases are licensed via Case marking, or K-government, but heads are licensed via head movement and incorporation. Thus, movement of V to T, and incorporation of V and T, as in (72), is sufficient to make T visible. On the other hand, movement of V to T is necessary (at some level of representation) in order for the visibility requirement on T to be satisfied. Here I will not try to take this matter any further, noting only that the problem of incorporation as a visibility relation holds in general for the class of N incorporations in Baker 1988.

Assuming that Locality theory is on the right track, there are consequences to be derived from it concerning not only the interaction of *wh*-islands with Tense, but also multiple *wh*-islands. Consider, for example, (73). Contrary to (66) and (70), sentences of this type, where an argument *wh*-phrase is extracted out of two *wh*-islands, are ill formed in Italian as well as in English.

(73) *[Che compito]$_i$ non sai   [a quale studente]$_j$ si chiedano
       which assignment don't you know to which student   they wonder
       [perchè$_k$ abbiamo assegnato t$_i$ t$_j$ t$_k$]
       why we gave

The approach suggested by Chomsky (1986a) is that the crossing of two CP barriers in (73) violates Subjacency, even though the two barriers are crossed in successive steps rather than in one step. But such a cumulative mechanism appears yet again to represent an ad hoc enrichment of the theory.

I propose instead that the relevant generalization concerning the contrast between (66)/(70) and (73) is that two and only two movement tracks are available in the grammar. Two different categories can move along these two different tracks, but a third category has no route available and cannot move at all. This generalization follows from Locality theory, where the two escape routes are represented by the formation of a categorial index sequence and an address-based sequence, respectively. If this is correct, then the contrast between (66)/(70) and (73) directly supports the theory. Consider the relevant substructure of (73), as in (74).

(74)

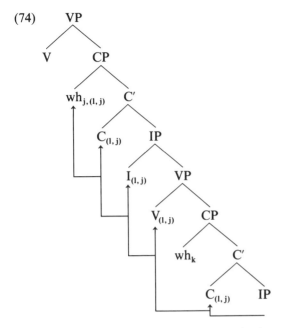

The lower CP in (74) corresponds to the lowest embedded CP in (73); thus, wh_k corresponds to *perchè*. The higher CP in (74) corresponds to the intermediate CP in (73); thus, $wh_{j,(l,j)}$, where we assume that (l, j) is the address of wh_j, corresponds to *a quale studente*. Movement of the adjunct *perchè* to the embedded Spec of CP in (74) of course satisfies antecedent government. Similarly, the subsequence (C, I, V, C) of address (l, j) in (74) satisfies the government requirement for *a quale studente*. However, consider the third argument to be moved, *che compito*. Movement via categorial coindexing is blocked in (74) by the fact that the Spec of both CPs is already filled, so that the argument is forced to cross CP barriers, violating Locality. Movement via an address-based sequence is also blocked in (74), by the fact that all heads are already addressed, so that a number of barriers must be crossed and Locality is violated again. If this argument is correct, then Locality theory predicts all sentences of the form in (73) to be ill formed without any need for further stipulation.

Now notice that in (73) all three *wh*-phrases involved are extracted from the most deeply embedded CP; thus, their three extraction trajectories all overlap at some point in the tree. It is possible to construct sentences where again three *wh*-phrases are involved and one *wh*-phrase is extracted over two *wh*-islands, but only two trajectories overlap at any given point in the tree. It is easy to show that Locality theory predicts such sentences to be grammatical; indeed, in my judgment the relevant examples, as in (75), contrast with (73).

(75) [Che compito]$_i$ non sai   [perchè$_j$ si chiedano
     which assignment don't you know why   they wonder
     [[a quale studente]$_k$ abbiamo assegnato t$_i$ t$_k$] t$_j$]
     to which student   we gave

The crucial indexed substructure for (75) is as in (76).

(76)

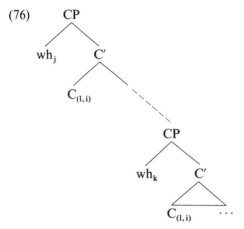

The higher and lower CPs in (76) represent the intermediate and most embedded CPs in (75), respectively. Thus, *wh*$_k$ corresponds to *a quale studente* and *wh*$_j$ to *perchè*. I have assumed that both *wh*-phrases in (76) move by categorial coindexing, which of course is allowed by the fact that their chains do not overlap at any point. If so, the third *wh*-phrase, *che compito*, an addressed category—say, of address (*l, i*)—is free to move via an address-based sequence, which can include both of the C heads in (76), as indicated. Hence, any sentence of the type in (75) is predicted to be well formed. In short, Locality theory allows us to derive the following empirical result: the extraction paths of any two *wh*-phases can overlap at any point in a tree, but the paths of three or more cannot. It is important to stress that the theory was not originally designed to encompass this prediction. On the contrary, as far as I know, no such empirical generalization has previously been proposed. Thus, the fact that this result follows from the theory must be counted as an argument in its favor.

The obvious qualification to this discussion is that the data themselves are potentially controversial. Rizzi (1980) judges all sentences where a *wh*-phrase crosses two *wh*-islands to be ungrammatical. But none of the examples that he gives are of the type in (73); I believe that the decisive fact in this argument is the contrast between (75) and (73). On the other hand, Rizzi (1980) finds a contrast between sentences like (77), which he judges well formed, and sentences like (78), which he judges ill formed. In (77)–(78), exactly as in (66)/(70), two *wh*-phrases are extracted, though three rather than two levels of embedding are involved; the only difference between (77) and (78) is the landing site of the lower *wh*-phrase. Locality theory predicts no contrast between (77) and (78), and indeed predicts that both should be well formed; my own judgments are consistent with this prediction.

(77) Gianni, [a cui]$_i$ ritengo [che tu sappia [[che cosa]$_j$
      Gianni, to whom I believe that you know   what
      io voglia regalare t$_j$ t$_i$]]. . .
      I want to give

(78) Gianni, [a cui]$_i$ non so   [[che cosa]$_j$ tu ritenga [che
      Gianni, to whom I don't know   what   you believe that
      io voglia regalare t$_j$ t$_i$]]
      I want to give

    If true, these data are directly relevant for the theory proposed by Pesetsky (1982). Well-formed examples of the type in (75) indeed conform to the Path Containment Condition, according to which overlapping extraction paths must be nested inside one another. On the other hand, the crucially ill formed (73) also conforms to the same principle. Indeed, under Pesetsky's (1982) assumptions, the adjunct dependency is nested inside the indirect object dependency, which in turn is nested inside the direct object dependency. (73) then provides a clear argument that the Path Containment Condition is insufficient. Whether the Path Containment Condition is also unnecessary is of course an altogether different question. Indeed, Locality theory apparently cannot derive the various crossing path effects noted by Pesetsky (1982). Thus, the Path Containment Condition remains fundamentally unassimilated to Locality. A possible reason is that, contra Pesetsky (1982), crossing constraints are truly linear in nature and must be imputed to some independent component of the grammar. Here, however, I leave this issue essentially open.

    Finally, let us return to the interaction of *wh*-islands with Tense islands. In order for the interaction of a *wh*-island and a Tense island to produce ungrammatically it is necessary that the Tense island be contained in the *wh*-island. This is indeed the case in ill-formed examples like (67). Well-formed example like (66) also contain a *wh*-island and a Tense island, but crucially the *wh*-island is contained in the Tense island. Consider then the relevant structure for the extraction in (66), as in (79), where we assume that the address of wh_i (namely, *what*) is (k, i), and that the address of T_1 is (m, l).

(79)

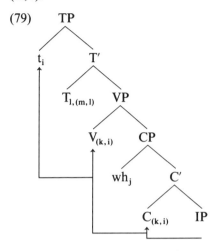

In (79) the embedded Spec of CP position is filled by wh_j, corresponding to *how* in (66). This prevents any other *wh*-phrase from moving out of the embedded CP via categorial coindexing. Thus, the only extraction path left open for wh_i, *what*, is the address-based path. Indeed, in (79) there is a well-formed subsequence (V, C) of address (k, i) through which extraction from CP can take place. On the other hand, since the T head in (79) has independent denotation and hence an address of its own, the subsequence cannot be extended to include T. If we take the latter to be the only possible derivation, as the discussion so far apparently forces us to, then (66) is incorrectly predicted to be ungrammatical. An alternative derivation is possible, however, which is indicated in (79). This breaks the address-based sequence at V and continues with a sequence based on the categorial index i of *what*. Thus, on the basis of a mixed address-based and categorial index sequence the theory predicts the well-formedness of (66).

Notice that the logic of this discussion of Tense islands also points toward the general conclusion that although address-based dependencies are sensitive to them, categorial index dependencies are not. The theoretical basis for this is clear. Although T is an argument of V and is addressed by it, the phrase it heads, TP, is not an argument. Thus, TP can be associated with an Ā-position, as in (79), making it transparent for categorial index dependencies. This is the reverse of the situation encountered with *wh*-islands, where no Ā-escape hatch is available for categorial index dependencies, but the head remains transparent for address-based ones.

Thus, Locality theory turns out to have another property that distinguishes it from other current theories. As in other theories, there are islands that all types of dependencies obey, including complex NP islands and all Subjacency islands, and there are islands that only categorial index dependencies obey, including *wh*-islands and in general Relativized Minimality islands. However, there is at least one type of island that address-based dependencies are sensitive to, but not categorial index dependencies: namely, Tense islands. Other theories are constructed so that the latter situation never arises. Locality theory therefore reveals a deeper symmetry where other theories see only a superficial asymmetry.

On the other hand, a problem arises when the results obtained in this section and in the previous one are compared. In this section I have concluded that Tense islands deprive arguments of the address-based strategy for extraction, forcing them into the Spec-to-Spec strategy; this correctly predicts that they are sensitive to *wh*-islands. In the previous section I have reconstructed within my theory the generalization in Rizzi's (1990) Relativized Minimality to the effect that *wh*-islands and pseudo-opacity or inner islands have the same properties with respect to extractions. The problem is that if embedding a Tense island inside a *wh*-island creates a configuration where extraction is degraded with respect to its untensed *wh*-island counterpart, we expect that embedding a Tense island inside a pseudo-opacity or inner island will produce a comparable effect. However, I know of no data that support this prediction.

Unless more sophisticated data are found that do support it, the failure of this prediction can be taken to indicate some failure of the theory. However, a whole range of data also indicate that the treatment of Tense islands under Locality theory is correct: for instance, their interaction with adjunct islands, discussed in section 3.5, or their interaction with long-distance binding, discussed in chapter 4. Furthermore, Frampton's (1990) data show that a Tense island need not be immediately dominated by another island (*wh*-island or other) in order for them to interact, as Locality theory indeed predicts. I will then tentatively assume that the argument in favor of address-based dependencies provided by Tense islands goes through as before, and I will leave any other residual problems open for future discussion.

3.4   (Definite) DP Islands

In previous discussion we have derived the properties of phrasal extraction from nominals on the basis of the most elementary conception of their structure, invoking no level of functional projection above NP. In what follows we will systematically translate these conclusions concerning nominals into a framework that includes at least one functional projection above NP—namely, DP—at the same time extending them to a wider range of examples.

First consider complex NP islands. As we have seen, current theories of locality have difficulty in accounting for violations with CPs in the object position of N, as in (80)–(81).

(80) *Who$_i$ did you see [many attempts [to portray t$_i$]]

(81) *How$_i$ did you see [many attempts [to portray them t$_i$]]

Given Locality theory, these can be correctly predicted under the simple assumption that heads that are themselves addressed do not let other addresses pass through. If so, when an addressed NP is extracted from, an address-based sequence cannot include its head N, which is differently addressed by percolation; and Locality is violated.

Next consider how the theory can be extended if we assume a framework in which every NP is associated with a functional projection DP. If complex NP islands are to be derived under Locality theory as before, at least one of the two heads, N or D or both, must be addressed when the DP is. One possibility is that both heads are addressed, as indicated in (82). Deriving complex NP islands for address-based sequences is then straightforward, since the D and N heads in (82) cannot enter an address-based dependency, leading to a violation of locality.

(82)

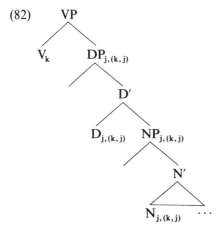

Let us consider the consequences of adopting the structure in (82) for antecedent government. Under a theory of adjunctions of the type adopted by Chomsky (1986a), at least DP in (82) cannot be adjoined to, because it is an argument. For the same reason, under our revised framework of assumptions, DP cannot be associated with an $\bar{\text{A}}$-position. This in turn means that DP necessarily represents a barrier for antecedent government, as desired. Thus, adopting (82) does not involve any modification of our theory of complex NP islands in this respect.

Next let us consider extractions from NP-internal positions. One fundamental fact about these cases is that adjuncts are not extractable, as in (83).

(83) *[With what kind of sleeves]$_i$ did you buy [many sweaters t$_i$]

Under Locality theory, this must mean again that antecedent government cannot be satisfied across a DP and an NP. As before, under Chomsky's (1986a) theory of adjunctions, this result is automatically achieved by assuming that adjunction to DP is impossible because DP is an argument. Under our revised theory, the same result is obtained by assuming that only nonarguments, and hence not DP, can be associated with an $\bar{\text{A}}$-position. If so, DP constitutes an absolute barrier for antecedent government, as desired.

The fact that extraction of arguments from DP-internal position is possible at all, as in (84), must mean, on the other hand, that address-based dependencies formed across N and D can be well formed, apparently contradicting the conclusion that we have just reached for complex NP islands.

(84) Who$_i$ did you see [pictures of t$_i$]

However, the extraction of arguments of N does appear to be constrained in ways in which the extraction of arguments of V is not. In particular, although extraction from the indefinite nominal in (84) is permitted, extraction from the definite nominals in (85)–(86) is not.

(85) *Who$_i$ did you see [these pictures of t$_i$]

(86) *Who$_i$ did you see [every picture of t$_i$]

Thus, a definiteness constraint appears to hold, which is again not predicted by current locality theories. What appears to be crucially involved in this constraint is a property of the head D. Now, what sets Locality theory apart from other locality theories is its ability to predict islands created by heads, and specifically denotational heads. In this way, it predicts not only complex NP islands, but also Tense islands. The question then is whether it can predict that an island is created by definite Ds as well, as opposed to indefinite ones.

Of course, under Locality theory, in order for a definite D to create an island, it is necessary for it to be addressed. Indeed, so far we have assumed that DPs are associated with indexed structures of the type in (82), where DP is assigned an address and transmits it to its head D. However, in (82) we have assumed that both NP and N are addressed as well. Suppose that this is not necessarily the case, and that whereas DP and D are addressed, NP and N are not, as in (87).

(87)

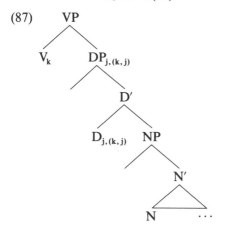

(87) is equivalent to saying that the argumental, or denotational, head of DP is D, whereas NP functions simply as a predicate of D. Remember that under the assumption that NP is not associated with any functional projection, we concluded that the only possibility for an argument of N to be extracted resides in the ability of N to address its argument by assigning it its address, rather than its categorial index. If D is addressed but not N, as in (87), then this possibility disappears, along with any escape route for arguments of N. Thus, if definite Ds are associated with the addressing structure in (87), the theory predicts that, as in (85)–(86), they are absolute barriers for extraction.

Next consider indefinite NPs, as in (84). The analysis that Locality theory requires is clear. We must assume that although definite DPs can be associated only with the addressing structure in (87), indefinite DPs can be associated with the addressing structure in (82), where the address of DP is transmitted not just to D but also to NP and N. Consider then the addressed structure relevant for (84), as in (88).

(88)   VP

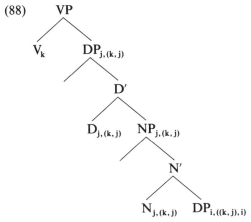

In (88) the higher DP is addressed by V, as indicated; the lower DP, corresponding to the trace of *who* in (84), is addressed by N, corresponding to *pictures*. In particular, in (88) the lower DP is assigned an address corresponding, not to the categorial index of N, but to its address; hence, the lower DP has an address that includes the address of N. This means that under extraction the lower DP is able to form an address-based sequence with N and D, the requirement on (address-based) sequences being not that their members have identical indices, but rather that their members have compatible indices, where compatibility of indices is in turn defined in terms of inclusion.

Remember that in the case of a definite DP, the intuitive content of a structure like (87) is that the argumental, or denotational, head is D, and that NP functions as a predicate of it. What the addressing structure for an indefinite DP as in (88) intuitively implies is that the whole DP functions as an argument, or a denotational unit. Indeed, we can assume that the structure in (87) is also possible for an indefinite; but what is crucial for the possibility of extracting one of its arguments is that (87) is not necessary.

Locality theory can also be argued to predict that the class of Ds that necessitate the structure in (87) both create an absolute barrier for movement, as in (84), and at the same time make their DPs sensitive to *wh*-islands under extraction, as in (10), repeated here.

(10) *[OGNI DICHIARAZIONE]$_i$, mi chiedo [perchè$_j$
       every statement,   I wonder   why
       abbia ritrattato t$_i$ t$_j$]
       he retracted

This is because it is precisely those cases where D is the denotational head that can be assumed to require movement of D at LF, creating a variable in D position. The *wh*-island violation then arises because all head movement, of which D-raising is an instance, must satisfy Locality through categorial index sequences, or in practice antecedent government. The cases in which the whole DP is a denotational unit, on the other hand, as in (82), can be assumed to correspond to LF representations where no D-raising has taken place, but where the whole DP corresponds to a variable. No *wh*-island violation will then arise in these cases if the DP itself is addressed. Interestingly, the correlation between definiteness and sensitivity to *wh*-islands under extraction breaks down with demonstratives, as seen by the contrast in grammaticality between (86) and (89).

(89) [QUESTE DICHIARAZIONI]$_i$, mi chiedo [perchè$_j$
       these statements,   I wonder   why
       abbia ritrattato t$_i$ t$_j$]
       he retracted

This discrepancy is easily explained, however. The demonstrative in (86) and (89) has denotational properties and makes DP into an absolute barrier for movement in (86). But of course its reference does not depend on an operator-variable structure at LF; hence, DP itself displays no sensitivity to *wh*-islands, as in (89), since D-raising need not take place.

Because the structure of DPs has been dictated so far by the needs of the proposed theory of extractions, it is worth considering briefly whether it is appropriate on purely phrase-structural grounds. The NP portion of (82) or (87) is unproblematic; its head N represents the nominal head of the construction, and the A-positions under N' and NP can be filled by the arguments of N. We can furthermore assume that articles and quantifiers alike are Ds. Pronouns can also occupy the D position; indeed in languages such as French and Italian pronominal clitics have essentially the same morphology as definite articles. This of course fits with the hypothesis that D can be the denotational head in DP.

Finally, if all extraction from NP-internal position is address-based, as under the Locality approach, it immediately follows that such extraction is not sensitive to antecedent government islands, in particular, *wh*-islands. This prediction appears to be correct, as in (90).

(90) Who$_i$ do you wonder [how$_j$ to collect [pictures of t$_i$] t$_j$]

Notably, this is the reverse of the prediction made by theories of the type proposed by Kayne (1981a) and Cinque (1991) under which an N simply has defective (head-)governing properties with respect to V. Indeed, if the heart of the matter is that a nominal head is not a "proper governor," then a complement of the head should behave essentially like an adjunct under extraction; but it does not. I have stressed so far the advantages of the proposed theory of extraction across N in terms of explanatory adequacy; to this can now be added the apparent empirical inadequacy of alternative theories like Kayne's (1981a) and Cinque's (1991) with respect to (90).

Apart from predicting that denotational heads create islands, Locality theory differs from other theories of locality in not allowing for a potentially infinite number of escape routes. Instead, we have seen that it predicts that a double *wh*-extraction is allowed, if one *wh*-phrase takes the antecedent government path and the other *wh*-phrase the address path; but a triple *wh*-extraction is impossible, since no third path is available. Next consider extraction from DPs. We have seen in (90) that an argument of N can be extracted across a *wh*-island. The Italian examples in (91)–(92) show that two different arguments of the same N can be successfully extracted out of a *wh*-island, one at a time.

(91) [Di che papa]$_i$ non sai   [dove$_j$ trovare [un ritratto t$_i$
     of which pope do you wonder where to find   a portrait
     di Raffaello] t$_j$]
     of Raphael

(92) [Di che pittore]$_i$ non sai   [dove$_j$ trovare
     of which painter do you wonder where to find
     [un ritratto di Giulio II t$_i$] t$_j$]
     a portrait of Julius II

It is true that a number of theories specifically exclude sentences of the type in (91), including Aoun's (1985), and before it Cinque's (1980) and Chomsky's (1973). Under all of these theories, (91), or its French or English counterpart, violates the Specified Subject Condition (SSC). The well-formedness of (91), confirmed in French by Milner (1985), can however be used to argue against the relevance of the SSC for *wh*-movement. If this conclusion is valid, then in turn a pivotal argument in favor of Aoun's (1985) theory of locality is eliminated.

The same argument that the SSC is irrelevant to extraction from NPs is made by Pollock (1989b), on the basis of examples structurally (though not thematically) identical to (91). According to Pollock (1989b), the correct generalization concerning extraction from NPs is that an object of N can be extracted in the presence of a subject, but only if it is a possessor

subject. This contrasts with the SSC-type generalization proposed by
Cinque (1980), according to which an object of N cannot be extracted in
the presence of a subject. It is not clear, however, that even Pollock's
(1989b) restriction is necessary. On the one hand, in Romance two geni-
tives are not allowed unless one of them is a possessive. Thus, (93) appears
not to be (fully) grammatical, as opposed to the (fully) grammatical (94).
Given this fact, there is simply no source for multiple arguments in NP in
the absence of a possessor.

(93) *Il furto   dell'icona   del custode
      the theft of the icon of the custodian

(94)   Il furto   dell'icona   da parte del custode
       the theft of the icon by the custodian
       (lit. 'on the part of the custodian')

On the other hand, extracting an object of N in the presence of a subject
in English implies extracting it from a definite DP, as in (95), since geni-
tives imply definiteness.

(95) *[Of which pope]$_i$ did you see [Raphael's portrait t$_i$]

Hence, the ungrammaticality of (95) is independently explained under
Locality theory as a violation of a definite D island.

    Let us now consider what happens if two arguments of N are *wh*-
extracted at once. Locality theory predicts ill-formedness, since of the two
extraction paths normally available in a sentence (the antecedent government path and the address path), only one (the address path) is available
in a DP. This prediction turns out to be correct, as in (96)–(97).

(96) *[Di che pittore]$_i$ ti chiedi   [[di che papa]$_j$ abbia visto
       of which painter do you wonder   of which pope I saw
       [un ritratto t$_j$ t$_i$]]
       a portrait

(97) *[Di che papa]$_i$ ti chiedi   [[di che pittore]$_j$ abbia visto
       of which pope do you wonder   of which painter I saw
       [un ritratto t$_i$ t$_j$]]
       a portrait

Of course, the correct prediction with respect to (96)–(97) also follows
from theories like Kayne's (1981a) and Cinque's (1991), since in the absence of proper (head) government by N, arguments of N are essentially
on a par with adjuncts. Remember however that the same theories predict
a comparable ill-formedness when just one argument of N is extracted

across a *wh*-island—incorrectly, since examples of this type are well formed, as in (91)–(92). To repeat, then, Locality theory appears to be empirically superior to the alternatives, quite apart from the fact that under this theory, the difference between the government properties of V heads and the government properties of N heads also follows from general principles, and not from stipulation.

3.5 Selective Island Sensitivity

So far, Locality theory has been based entirely on the locality principle formulated in chapter 2. The notion of barrier used in this theory in turn represents the conjunction of two different types of requirement. On the one hand, there is a minimality requirement, in the sense of Chomsky (1986a), under which a maximal projection is a barrier for all positions it dominates, except its head and its Spec. On the other hand, there is a g-marking requirement, a reconstruction of the L-marking requirement of Chomsky (1986a), under which a maximal projection must be sister to a head.

Interestingly, in other theories—say, Chomsky's (1986a) or Rizzi's (1990)—only nonarguments are sensitive to minimality. However, one of the chief contentions in this book is that the minimality requirement included in the notion of barrier proposed in chapter 2 applies to arguments and nonarguments alike. In the case of nonarguments, which must form categorial index dependencies, the minimality requirement accounts for *wh*-islands, exactly like Chomsky's (1986a) antecedent government or Rizzi's (1990) Relativized Minimality. In the case of arguments, which can move by forming address-based dependencies, the minimality requirement derives islands created by the intervention of an addressed head, such as complex NP islands, Tense islands, and so on. Thus, the minimality requirement embedded in the proposed notion of barrier affects all movement types, exactly as the L-marking or g-marking requirement that accounts for Subjacency islands in the theories of Chomsky (1986a) and Rizzi (1990), as well as in Locality theory.

Since we have concentrated on minimality islands in this chapter, let us consider subject and adjunct islands again. Parasitic gaps cannot be included in the present discussion, since they involve a number of complications extraneous to the main line of argumentation here. They are dealt with in terms of Locality theory in Manzini 1991c. The crucial structure for subject island violations is shown in (98), the crucial structures for

adjunct island violations in (99). By contrast, (100) illustrates the crucial
structure for extraction from object constituents.

(98)
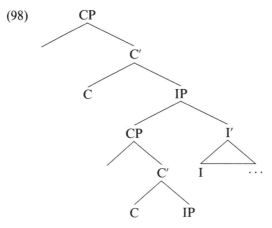

(99)
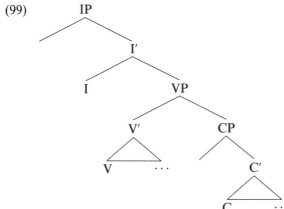

(100)
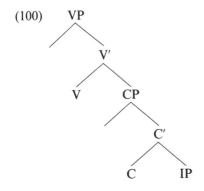

The core of both Chomsky's (1986a) L-marking proposal and of the g-marking proposal under discussion here is that subjects and adjuncts are islands because they do not have a sister relation to the head of the constituent they are embedded in. With respect to all of the configurations in (98)–(100), the Locality approach and Chomsky's (1986a) are, as we have seen, empirically equivalent.

Next consider the third main type of islands derived by Chomsky's (1986a) Subjacency: relative clause islands. According to Chomsky (1986a), relative clause islands are a subtype of adjunct islands. Indeed, the relevant structure for a relative clause island violation is assumed to be as in (101), with N/D projections substituted for the matrix V/I projections in (99).

(101)

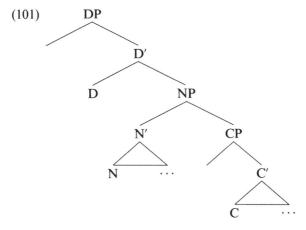

Given (101), Locality theory is again exactly equivalent to Chomsky's (1986a) theory. Remember, however, that under the latter theory, although relative clause islands could be derived under Subjacency, other complex NP island violations could not be derived. By contrast, Locality theory can now derive complex NP island violations for CPs that are objects of N as well as for relative clauses. This effectively means that this theory can derive relative clause islands whether relative clauses are attached as adjuncts, as in (101), or as complements of N.

Consider a typical complex NP configuration where CP is a complement of N, as in (102).

(102)   VP

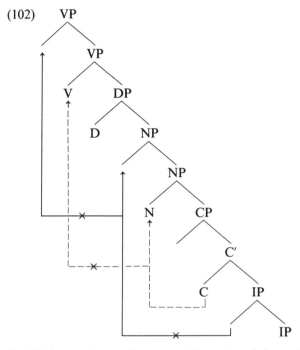

If a CP-internal trace forms an address-based dependency, then there can
be no well-formed link of the dependency above N, because at least D is
independently addressed, and a (V, N) link, as indicated, violates government. If the CP in (102) is taken to be a relative clause, this predicts
relative clause island violations with address-based dependencies. If on the
other hand a CP-internal trace in (102) forms a categorial index dependency, then extraction from the relative clause island in (102) is excluded for
at least two reasons, independently of the attachment of CP, not only
under Locality theory but under all current theories. The first reason is
that at least DP is an argument, and hence not associated with an Ā-escape
hatch, so that a barrier, DP, is crossed, even if NP is not an argument and
can be adjoined to, as indicated. The second reason is of course that every
relative clause is a *wh*-island; thus, the Spec of CP in (102) is filled by a
wh-operator, forcing the CP barrier to be crossed as well.

  In short, it is one of the consequences of Locality theory that it does not
force an adjunct-like attachment for relative clauses; rather, relative
clauses can be attached as complements of N, as in (102), and the impossibility of extracting not only adjuncts, but also arguments, still follows.
Notice in turn that although the sister position of a head is restricted to
the complements of that head in Chomsky's (1981) account, the only

motivation for such a restriction is that it prevents raising from subject into object position. But if for instance we commit ourselves to binary branching, as suggested by Kayne (1981b) and Larson (1988), among others, then raising to object appears to be independently excluded, since it necessarily produces a ternary branching configuration. If the relevant restriction proposed by Chomsky (1981) is abandoned, then the attachment of relative clauses as complements and their attachment as adjuncts appear to be equally possible.

Next let us reconsider the canonical configurations for Subjacency violations in (98) and (99). Remember that an important motivation for Kayne's (1983) definition of g-projections in terms of canonical government is that although violations of the subject constraint always produce unequivocally ungrammatical results, as in (103), this is not necessarily the case for violations of the adjunct constraint, as in (104).

(103)   *A doctor who$_i$ [[consulting t$_i$] bothered me]

(104)   (*)A doctor who$_i$ [I felt better [after consulting t$_i$]]

Thus, Kayne's (1983) notion of g-projection is designed to derive the subject constraint, since subjects are on a non–canonically ordered left branch, but not the adjunct constraint.

The alternative solution that I want to propose for the contrast in (103)–(104), is based on the conclusions just reached concerning relative clauses. (105) is a relevant example.

(105)   *The doctor who$_i$ I know [a suitable gift [to give to t$_i$]]

If the preceding discussion is correct, relative clauses can equally well be attached as adjuncts or as complements of N. In both cases government ensures that relative clause island violations are ungrammatical, as in (105). Furthermore, the possibility of attaching as complements is never open to subjects, since in a right-branching language, right branches can be complements or not, but left branches are necessarily noncomplements, whence the ill-formedness of (103). Let us consider the crucial case of adjuncts, as in (104). What we need to say is that adjuncts can attach as adjuncts proper, as in (99), in which case they cannot be extracted from; or, to the extent that they can be reanalyzed as complements, as in (100), they can be extracted from with (relatively) well-formed results.

One question that arises at this point is what elements exactly can be (marginally) extracted from adjunct islands. One possible generalization is that the contrast between address-based and categorial index dependencies is again involved. Another is proposed, however, by Cinque

(1991). Consider for instance subcategorized PPs, which are clearly ad-dressed under Locality theory, and which indeed, theory-neutrally, have the basic properties of addressed elements, such as extractability from *wh*-islands. According to Cinque (1991), these cannot be extracted from adjuncts any more than other adjuncts can; thus, the relevant generaliza-tion is that DPs, rather than addressed (or referential) elements, are (mar-ginally) extractable from selected islands. My own judgments regarding examples like (106) in a non-P-stranding language like Italian is that they are at worst intermediate in status between extractions like (104) and adjunct extractions like (107), which are indeed (strongly) ill formed.

(106) (*)L'avvocato [a cui]ᵢ   mi sono sentito meglio
      the lawyer   to whom I felt better
      [dopo essermi rivolto tᵢ]
      after turning

(107) *A reason whyᵢ I felt better [after consulting my doctor tᵢ]

Finally, (apparent) adjunct island violations are sensitive to Tense. Thus, (108) is ill formed with respect to (104); correspondingly, (103) and (105) are further degraded if the subject or relative clause is tensed.

(108) *The book whichᵢ my students took the exam [after they read tᵢ]

Although such a Tense effect remains mysterious under other frameworks, it is precisely what Locality theory predicts on the assumption that an address-based dependency is involved. Remember that under the assump-tions of this theory a T head can and must be made visible, and hence addressed, via incorporation. As a result, the theory predicts that the extraction sequence in (108) cannot include the T head embedded under the adjunct CP, because T has an address of its own; whence a locality violation.

To sum up: From a theoretical point of view, the conclusions reached in this chapter simply consolidate the results of the previous chapter. The only systematic innovation introduced here is a modification of the theory of movement—that is, of $\bar{\text{A}}$-escape hatches, as in (47)–(48). From an empirical point of view, on the other hand, I would contend that all of the desiderata listed in table 1.4 now follow from Locality theory. Table 3.1 reproduces those desiderata, together with the section in this chapter where the predictions are discussed and, as I would argue, are derived by the theory.

Table 3.1
Final island predictions

	Categorial index dependency	Address-based dependency
Subject island	* (3.5)	* (3.5)
Adjunct island	* (3.5)	* (3.5)
Relative clause island	* (3.5)	* (3.5)
(Complex) NP island	* (3.4)	* (3.4)
Definiteness island	* (3.4)	* (3.4)
Overlapping *wh*-islands	* (3.3)	* (3.3)
Wh-island	* (3.2)	OK (3.2)
Inner island	* (3.2)	OK (3.2)
Pseudo-opacity island	* (3.2)	OK (3.2)
Factive island	* (3.2)	OK (3.2)
Tense island	OK (3.3)	* (3.3)

Chapter 4
Locality Theory for Binding

4.1 Unification of Locality Theory for Movement and Binding

We have seen that Locality correctly predicts the locality behavior of A-traces; thus, as far as A-traces are concerned, this principle subsumes Binding Condition A in Chomsky's (1981) sense. The question then arises whether it can subsume the binding theory in its entirety; in other words, whether it correctly predicts the locality behavior of lexical anaphors and pronouns as well.

Consider Binding Condition A, in the formulation given in chapter 2. One preliminary difficulty in completely unifying it with Locality is that the domains of application of the two principles differ. Binding Condition A applies to anaphors; Locality applies to traces. Under Chomsky's (1981, 1982) theory, empty categories are divided into four major classes: anaphors, pronominals, referential expressions, and pronominal anaphors, which correspond, respectively, to A-traces, pro's, Ā-traces, and PRO's. Under this theory, the domains of application of Binding Condition A and Locality overlap, in that they both include A-traces; but they are irreducible to one another. On the other hand, under the theory espoused by Aoun (1985) and Brody (1985), all empty categories are anaphors. If so, the domain of application of Binding Condition A—namely, anaphors—subsumes the domain of application of Locality—namely, traces; hence, one potential obstacle to unification is removed.

Of course, the assumption that traces are anaphors is essentially ad hoc, in that apart from allowing for the unification of locality theory, it has no independent motivation. A weaker assumption thus appears preferable, under which anaphors and traces remain disjoint classes, but in turn belong to a superclass of, say, dependent elements. This allows us to formulate a minimal revision of Locality, under which the requirement it expresses applies to dependent elements, rather than to traces only, as in (1).

(1) *Locality*

If α is a dependent element, there is an antecedent β for α, and a sequence $(\beta, \dots, \alpha)$ that satisfies government.

In practice, when applied to lexical anaphors, Chomsky's (1986a) Binding Condition A derives data of the type in (2), where *himself* can be locally bound by the embedded subject but cannot be long-distance bound by the matrix subject.

(2) Peter$_i$ thinks that John$_j$ likes himself$_{*i/j}$

Obviously, if (1) is to represent the unified theory of locality for movement and anaphor binding, then (2) and similar examples must be shown to follow from it.

The first question that arises is whether lexical anaphors have a categorial index and/or an address. The conception of categorial indices as indices of lexical content entails the view that lexical anaphors have a categorial index of their own. Thus, the parallelism between categorial indices and standard (referential) indices breaks down in this respect, for under standard assumptions anaphors do not have (referential) indices of their own. Correspondingly, a problem arises for Locality theory if the formation of dependencies, or sequences, requires coindexing. Under standard theories, it is the absence of (referential) indices associated with lexical anaphors that allows them to be coindexed with their antecedents. Under Locality theory, if lexical anaphors must be associated with a categorial index of their own, they apparently cannot acquire one through coindexing. Instead, I propose that lexical anaphors are associated with a special type of categorial index, which I will refer to as a *variable categorial index*. Remember that the definition of sequence, originally formulated in terms of coindexing, was reformulated in chapter 2 in terms of compatibility of indices. Let us then assume that it is a property of variable categorial indices that they are compatible with any other categorial index; it follows that lexical anaphors can systematically enter into categorial index sequences with their antecedents, as desired. Since the notion of compatibility of indices has been defined in terms of inclusion, we can also formally state the basic property of variable categorial indices with respect to coindexing by saying that a variable categorial index includes any other index.

Let us then consider whether (1) derives the correct predictions concerning (2), given the categorial index structure in (3).

(3) Peter_i thinks that John_j likes himself_x

First consider the sequence (John_j, himself_x). Since the anaphor is in object position, VP is a barrier for it, and since its antecedent is in the Spec of IP position, government is apparently violated. However, this violation can be corrected if, as assumed in chapter 2 following Sportiche (1988), the Spec of IP position is a derived position for the subject, and its base-generated position is VP-internal. If so, it can be the trace of the subject in VP-internal position that binds the anaphor, thus correctly predicting that the subject is a possible antecedent for the anaphor. As for the sequence (Peter_i, himself_x), Locality obviously predicts it to be ill formed. Because this sequence crosses at least one barrier (the embedded sentence boundary CP), government is not satisfied, and Locality is violated.

The real challenge for Locality theory arises when we consider the second type of indices on the basis of which sequences can be formed, namely, addresses. Under the definition of addressing, *himself* in (2) is obviously addressed, since it is Case-marked by the head V. The crucial question is whether a dependency between *Peter* and *himself*, which cannot be established via categorial coindexing because of locality considerations, can nevertheless be established via coaddressing. If the relevant portion of the addressed structure corresponding to (2) is as in (4), there is a very simple reason why the answer is again negative, as desired— namely, that the anaphor *himself* and its potential antecedent *Peter* have different addresses. Thus, incompatibility of addresses prevents them from forming an address-based sequence.

(4) $\text{Peter}_{i,(j,i)}$ I_j thinks that John I likes_k $\text{himself}_{x,(k,x)}$

An interesting technical issue raised by the notion of compatibility of indices is whether *himself* and *John* in (2) do in fact have compatible or incompatible addresses. In particular, one can ask whether I, as a functional category associated with V, has a categorial index of its own or simply the categorial index of V itself, as suggested by the treatment of functional categories so far. Under the latter hypothesis, a structure of the type in (5) is obtained. But even in (5) we can assume that the addresses of *John* and *himself* are incompatible; hence, an address-based dependency cannot be established between the two.

(5) Peter I thinks that $\text{John}_{l,(k,l)}$ I_k likes_k $\text{himself}_{x,(k,x)}$

To sum up: If the preceding discussion is on the right track, lexical anaphors such as *himself* can only form categorial index dependencies. Thus, for *himself* and similar anaphors, Locality has the force of Binding Condition A, in that it allows objects to be bound from subject position, but not across sentence boundaries. Hence, if this line of reasoning is correct, Locality indeed subsumes Binding Condition A.

Thus, the conclusion that an anaphor such as *himself* cannot form an address-based sequence, because of the incompatibility between its address and its antecedent's address, is crucial to unifying Locality for movement and binding. Unfortunately, there is one outstanding problem for such a conclusion. This is that if PRO is not Case-marked, we expect it not to be addressed under Locality theory. Thus, we can expect a long-distance address-based sequence to exist between *himself* and a PRO, incorrectly predicting long-distance binding in examples like (6).

(6) *Peter$_i$ tried [PRO$_i$ to believe [that I liked himself$_x$]]

Here I will not attempt a solution, but will simply point out that the status of PRO with respect to Case marking and visibility is problematic quite independently of Locality theory, and of the use of Case marking and visibility to define addressing. The problem arises in particular in Chomsky's (1981, 1986b) theory with respect to what constitutes a visible head of a chain. Essentially two types of solutions can be envisaged. Either PRO is directly stipulated to be visible; or it is stipulated to receive some suitably abstract type of Case, so that visibility follows on standard Case-marking grounds. Of course, the second solution can be straightforwardly accepted into Locality theory, since the abstract Case of PRO, presumably related to nonfinite I, will be able to define an address for it. If so, the conclusion that anaphors can never enter address-based dependencies can be derived for examples like (6) as well. Hence, the unified formulation of Locality for movement and anaphor binding, as in (1), can ultimately be upheld.

Finally, the question arises whether there is a unified formulation of Locality that covers pronouns as well as anaphors. This of course corresponds to the familiar problem of the disjunction between Binding Conditions A and B. A way of eliminating this disjunction is simply to strengthen (1) to a biconditional, as in (7).

(7) *Locality*
     α is a dependent element iff there is an antecedent β for α and a
     sequence $(\beta, \ldots, \alpha)$ that satisfies government

The left-to-right reading of the biconditional yields (1). If on the other hand dependent elements are defined as traces and anaphors, the right-to-left reading of the biconditional is equivalent to the requirement that if α is not an anaphor or a trace, then it is not governed by any β it forms a sequence with. This differs from Binding Condition B only in that it affects nonanaphors rather than pronominals and therefore affects referential expressions as well. If referential expressions are independently required not to be bound, the requirement expressed by the right-to-left reading of (7) will simply be redundant with respect to them.

The pronominal data accounted for by Binding Condition B are of the type in (8) for the English pronoun *him*.

(8) Peter$_i$ thinks that John$_j$ likes him$_x$ $j \neq x$

These must now follow from (7), if (7) is to subsume Binding Condition B. In (8) the pronoun *him* can be bound long-distance by the matrix subject, but cannot be locally bound by the embedded one. Like the anaphor in (2), *him* has not only a variable categorial index but also an address. However, since its potential antecedents *Peter* and *John* are independently addressed, no address-based sequence can be formed. This leaves the two categorial index sequences (*Peter*, *him*) and (*John*, *him*). But the sequence (*John*, *him*) is ill formed under (7): given a government relation between *John* or its trace in VP-internal position and *him*, *him* is required to be an anaphor, which it is not. The alternative sequence (*Peter*, *him*) is well formed, since (7) allows nondependent elements to form sequences that do not satisfy government. Thus, the fundamental data concerning pronouns such as English *him* are indeed derived under (7).

It is important to stress that under Locality theory there is one and only one reason why lexical anaphors and pronouns pattern with such disparate elements as adjunct Ā-traces, head traces, and traces of A-movement in being subject to a more stringent definition of locality than argument Ā-traces. This has to do with the unavailability of address-based sequences in the former set of cases. Specifically, adjunct traces and A-traces cannot form address-based sequences because they are addressless; lexical pronouns and anaphors cannot do so because they and any potential antecedents have incompatible addresses. Furthermore, it is important to stress that the theory of indexing and locality that is being proposed here has been constructed and motivated entirely on the basis of movement. The fact that it can be extended to binding with only trivial modifications constitutes independent confirmation of its validity.

From an empirical point of view, only reflexives and pronouns corresponding to an object of V have been considered in (2) and (8). However, the correct predictions obviously follow from Locality theory with respect to the other major argument position as well, namely, the subject position, as in (9)–(10).

(9)   *John$_i$ thinks that $\left\{ \begin{array}{l} \text{heself}_x \\ \text{himself}_x \end{array} \right\}$ is unhappy

(10)   John$_i$ thinks that he$_x$ is unhappy

Since the anaphor and pronoun in (9)–(10) are addressed, they cannot form an address-based dependency with another addressed position. This restricts them to categorial index dependencies. The anaphor in (9) is therefore correctly predicted to be ill formed, since it cannot have an antecedent that governs it. Similarly, the pronoun in (10) is correctly predicted to be well formed, whatever its reading, again because there is no antecedent position from which it can be governed.

More interestingly, it is worth considering what the distribution of anaphors is predicted to be in adjunct position. Although anaphors and pronouns typically are in complementary distribution in argument position, as in (2) and (8)–(10), they typically are not in complementary distribution in adjunct position. Thus, *himself* is acceptable in English in the adjunct position in (11), but so is *him*, as in (12).

(11)   John$_i$ saw a snake near himself$_x$

(12)   John$_i$ saw a snake near him$_x$

Locality theory immediately accounts for the data in (11)–(12). If we adopt the structure for PPs that was proposed in chapter 2, *himself* and *him* are not addressed in (11)–(12) in the absence of V-P reanalysis and therefore cannot form an address-based dependency. However, they can form categorial index dependencies. The dependency (*John, himself*) is predicted to be ill formed, since it crosses a PP barrier and hence violates government; but the dependency (*John, him*) is predicted to be well formed, very much for the same reason. On the other hand, again following the discussion of movement from PPs in chapter 2, we can assume that a P head has no categorial index of its own and that the PP acquires a categorial index only by percolation from its object. If so, then the categorial dependencies (*John, near himself*) and (*John, near him*) can also be formed, where the whole PP is associated with the categorial index percolated from the anaphor or pronoun it contains. In this case, the pronoun dependency is ill formed, because no barrier intervenes between the two members of the dependency, so that it satisfies government; but very much for the same reason the anaphor dependency is well formed. Thus, the non-complementary distribution of *himself* and *him* in (11)–(12) is ultimately accounted for.

Notice also that the reason for the noncomplementary distribution of *himself* and *him* in (11)–(12) is exactly the same as the reason for the contrast between (13) and (14).

(13)   [Near whom]$_i$ did you see the snake t$_i$

(14)   *Who$_i$ did you see the snake [near t$_i$]

In (13) movement of the whole PP corresponds to the derivation that licenses the occurrence of *himself* in (11). In (14) movement of the DP embedded under PP corresponds to the derivation that licenses the occurrence of *him* in (12). Thus, the asymmetry between movement and binding in (11) versus (14) is only apparent. Furthermore, Locality theory predicts that although *himself*, or to be more precise *near himself*, can be bound by the immediately superordinate subject in (11), this does not represent a case of long-distance binding; hence, the anaphor could not be bound for instance by a higher subject. Again it appears that the crucial data, shown in (15), support Locality theory.

(15)   *Mary$_i$ said that John$_j$ saw a snake near herself$_x$

4.2   Binding into DPs

As part of the task of unifying locality, we have argued that binding is characterized by the same locality theory as movement. However, so far we have examined only sentential positions; DP-internal positions—that is, positions immediately dominated by a projection of N, or D—remain to be considered. According to Chomsky (1981), these positions provide one of the crucial arguments in favor of a definition of locality for binding that, unlike the definition of barrier proposed here or Chomsky's (1986a) definition, refers to the notion of subject.

Chomsky's (1981) Binding Condition A, as reformulated in a barriers format in chapter 2, states that given an anaphor α and a governing category γ for α, there must be a β such that β binds α and γ does not exclude β. Binding Condition B states that given a pronoun α and a binder β for α, there must be a governing category γ for α such that γ excludes β. Using the terms developed here, a governing category for α can be defined as a maximal projection that dominates α, a g-marker for α, and an (accessible) subject, on the assumption that the notion of g-marker reconstructs Chomsky's (1981) notion of governor. In other words, the definition of governing category β can be reconstructed as in (16), which is the definition of barrier proposed in chapter 2 with the added requirement that β must dominate a subject accessible to α. Under its simplest definition, the notion of accessibility to α reduces to that of c-command by α; it is this definition of the notion that we will tentatively adopt.

(16) β is a governing category for α iff β is a maximal projection, β dominates α, if α has a g-marker then β dominates the g-marker for α, and β dominates a subject accessible to α.

Now, returning to DP-internal positions, it is possible to argue that at least the binding of pronouns in DPs is better accounted for under the proposed definition of barrier than under Chomsky's (1981) definition of governing category, as in (16). Indeed, Chomsky (1986b) has already argued that the notion of accessibility, if not the notion of subject, is irrelevant for pronouns. As in Manzini 1991a, then, I will simply reconstruct this argument within Locality theory, as an argument in favor of the non-subject-based notion of barrier for pronouns.

First consider a pronoun in the subject position of an object DP, as in (17).

(17) The boys$_i$ saw [their$_x$ pictures] in the post office

We can of course identify the subject position with the Spec of DP. By the subject-based definition of locality, the embedded DP is not a governing category for the pronoun: on the assumption that the pronoun does not c-command itself and hence is not accessible to itself, DP contains no subject accessible to it. This in turn predicts, incorrectly, that *their* is disjoint in reference from *the boys*. If we instead analyze (17) using the definition of barrier proposed in chapter 2, we find that unfortunately, the pronoun in the Spec of DP is g-marked by the V that DP is an object of; hence, DP is not a barrier for it either, and *their* is again incorrectly predicted to be disjoint in reference from *the boys*.

However, there is a way to revise this notion of barrier so as to correctly predict the reference relations in (17). Suppose that the g-marker for a given element is only optionally taken into account in computing the locality domain for that element, as under the definition of barrier in (18).

(18) β is a barrier for α iff β is a maximal projection, β dominates α (and if α has a g-marker, β dominates the g-marker of α).

Under (18), the barrier for the pronoun in (17) is VP if its g-marker, V, is taken into account, whereas it is DP if its g-marker, V, is disregarded. Of course, under the latter alternative, the possibility of disjoint reference between *their* and *the boys* follows, as desired. On the other hand, for examples involving traces or anaphors, the consequences of making the g-marking requirement optional are null. If the g-marker is not taken into account, ill-formedness will result in some cases; but this is irrelevant, since the alternative derivation, under which it is taken into account, is allowed by (18) in all cases.

Next consider a pronoun in the subject position of a DP that is itself in subject position, as in (19).

(19) The boys$_i$ thought that [their$_x$ pictures] were on sale

The lack of disjoint reference in (19) between *their* and *the boys* is correctly predicted under the proposed definition of barrier. Indeed, DP is straight-forwardly a barrier for the pronoun, for the same reasons any subject is a barrier for movement. However, the results are different under the subject-based definition of governing category in (16). Based on this definition, the governing category for the pronoun in (19) is the matrix sentence. Indeed, if the pronoun does not c-command itself, and hence is not accessible to itself, there is no subject accessible to it in DP; hence, DP is not a governing category for it. Similarly, on the assumption that DP does not itself c-command the pronoun it contains, and hence is not accessible to it, the embedded sentence does not contain a subject accessible to the pronoun, and therefore is not a governing category for it. Thus, *their* and *the boys* are incorrectly predicted to be disjoint in reference.

Consider next an example like (20), where a pronoun is in the object position of a subject DP.

(20) The boys$_i$ thought that [pictures of them$_x$] were on sale

DP is of course a barrier for the pronoun in (20), very much as it is a barrier for movement from the same position; hence, *them* and *the boys* are correctly predicted not to be disjoint in reference under (18). On the other hand, since no subject is accessible to the pronoun except the subject of the matrix sentence, the matrix sentence is predicted to be the governing category for it under (16), and *them* and *the boys* are incorrectly predicted to be disjoint in reference.

Finally, consider a pronoun in the object position of a DP, where the DP is itself in object position, as in (21).

(21) The boys$_i$ saw [pictures of them$_x$] in the post office

Under (18), the embedded DP is a barrier for the pronoun, for the same reason that the embedded DP is a barrier for movement from the same position (in the absence of reanalysis); hence, *them* and *the boys* are correctly predicted not to be disjoint in reference. Under (16), on the other hand, the governing category for the pronoun is again the matrix sentence, since the DP has no subject, let alone a subject accessible to the pronoun; hence, *them* and *the boys* are incorrectly predicted to be disjoint in reference.

In short, pronouns can be successfully accounted for in terms of the proposed notion of barrier, provided the g-marking requirement is made optional, as in (18). But this immediately creates an empirical problem. Consider (22).

(22) John$_i$ believes him$_x$ to be happy

Here, the pronoun in the subject position of the exceptional Case marking sentence is of course disjoint in reference from the matrix subject. Yet under (18) nothing prevents us from disregarding the g-marker for the pronoun—namely, the matrix V—so that the ECM sentence is a barrier for it. If so, the pronoun is predicted not to be disjoint in reference from the matrix subject, contrary to fact.

There is, however, an obvious difference between the Spec of DP position filled by the pronoun in (17) or (19), and the Spec of IP position filled by the pronoun in (22). In (22) the pronoun receives Case from V; hence, for the purposes of Case assignment, assuming that Case assignment is constrained by government, the government domain of the pronoun cannot be the embedded IP, but must be the matrix VP. Suppose then that each given position is associated with one government domain (or barrier) and only one. This means that IP cannot be a barrier for the pronoun in (22) for the purposes of binding; hence, it is correctly predicted that *John* and *him* must be disjoint in reference in (22). The previous discussion of pronouns in the Spec of DP position remains unchanged, however, since Case assignment takes place from inside the DP, and hence nothing forces the choice of a wider government domain.

Notice that under Chomsky's (1986b) theory, where the notion of accessibility is not relevant for pronouns, the examples in (17) and (19) follow correctly without having recourse to the optionality of the governor, in that the Spec of DP is taken to be governed by D (or equivalently the Spec of NP is taken to be governed by N). But a similar solution within Locality theory would appear to amount to a stipulation. Furthermore, examples of the type in (20) also follow correctly under Chomsky's (1986b) theory. However, for examples of the type in (21) the pronoun is incorrectly predicted to be disjoint in reference from the matrix subject, because the notion of subject, if not of accessibility, remains relevant through the notion of complete functional complex.

In short, if the preceding arguments are correct, the notion of (accessible) subject, or even of complete functional complex, is best abandoned for pronouns. The question then arises whether there is any comparable evidence for anaphors. As is well known, in contexts of the type in (17) and (19)–(21), anaphors and pronouns are not in complementary distribution. For instance, (23), corresponding to (17), is also well formed.

(23) The boys$_i$ saw [each other's$_x$ pictures] in the post office

Locality theory straightforwardly predicts the grammaticality of (23). Indeed, *each other* is in the Spec of DP in (23), and hence in an escape hatch position. This effectively makes VP into the locality domain for *each other*, and its ability to corefer with *the boys* follows.

Next consider (24), with *each other* substituting for the pronoun in (19).

(24) The boys$_i$ thought that [each other's$_x$ pictures] were on sale

In this case there is apparently no explanation for the noncomplementary distribution of pronoun and anaphor. Indeed, if *each other* forms a categorial index dependency with *the boys* in (24), Locality is predicted to be violated, in that at least a CP barrier is crossed. Nor can an address-based dependency be formed between *the boys* and *each other*, since they belong to two different argumental complexes.

Similar problems arise with examples of the type in (25)–(26), corresponding to (20) and (21), respectively.

(25) The boys$_i$ thought that [pictures of each other$_x$] were on sale

(26) The boys$_i$ saw [pictures of each other$_x$] in the post office

Both (25) and (26) have one reading that is predicted to be grammatical. This is the reading under which the picturing is reciprocal, rather than the seeing or the thinking. Presumably this corresponds to *each other* being bound by an implicit argument subject within DP, which is in turn interpreted as coreferential with *the boys*. In the next section we will indeed see that this is the only reading available in Italian, and that Italian reciprocals clearly support a non-subject-based definition of locality for referential dependencies; thus, the Italian counterpart to (24) is also ill formed. Since the same appears not to be true in English, it is obvious that some enrichment of the theory is in order. One possibility is to simply follow Reinhart and Reuland (1991) in assuming that English anaphors are potentially ambiguous between an anaphoric construal proper and a logophoric construal, which is available by default when the anaphoric construal fails. If this is the case, then the problem can essentially be disregarded here.

4.3 Italian Reciprocals

An argument in favor of a barrier-based approach to locality, rather than a subject-based one, is provided by reciprocals in Italian, if not in English. In Italian, the reciprocal *l'uno l'altro* consists of two separable elements, *l'uno* 'the one' and *l'altro* 'the other'. *L'altro* is found in A-position like a lexical anaphor; *l'uno* behaves more like a floating quantifier. Configurations of the type in (27) are then created, where R_1 corresponds to the dependency between *l'uno* and its antecedent DP, and R_2 corresponds to the dependency between *l'altro* and DP.

(27) (DP ... l'uno ... l'altro)

    R_1 R_2

Notice that a dependency R_{1*} is presumably established at LF by movement of *l'uno* to take scope over DP, as in the abstract configuration in (28).

(28) [l'uno$_i$ [DP t$_i$ ... l'altro]]

    R_{1*} R_2

For locality purposes, however, it is easy to check that R_1 is equivalent to R_{1*}, if *l'uno* takes scope by adjoining to the first branching node dominating DP. Thus, for ease of exposition we will refer to R_1 in (27); but R_{1*} in (28) can be substituted for R_1, without prejudicing the argument. It is important to stress that the purpose of this section is not to give a full account of reciprocal constructions, either universally or for Italian. Rather, the issue is simply whether *l'uno l'altro* in NP-internal position requires a subject-based definition of locality or the definition of barrier proposed in (18). I will conclude, as in Manzini 1991a, b, that *l'uno* behaves according to (18).

First consider a DP in the object position of a sentence. *L'uno* can float either externally or internally to the DP. If *l'uno* floats in a position external to DP, the sentence is well formed. Relevant examples are of the type in (29).

(29) Quei pittori$_i$ ammirano l'uno$_x$ [i ritratti   dell'altro$_x$]
     those painters admire   the one the pictures of the other

(29) however does not choose among locality domains for *l'uno*. By the definition of barrier in (18), on the assumption that *l'uno* is external to DP, its locality domain is the matrix predicate. The subject *quei pittori* is then correctly predicted to be a possible antecedent for it. But the same correct prediction of course follows under a subject-based definition of governing category, since in this case the governing category for *l'uno* is straightforwardly defined by *quei pittori* itself.

Next consider the case, crucial to determining the locality domain for *l'uno*, where *l'uno* floats DP-internally. This is exemplified in (30).

(30) Quei pittori$_i$ ammirano [i ritratti   l'uno$_x$ dell'altro$_x$]
       those painters admire   the portraits the one of the other

Examples of this type give rise to contradictory judgments. Certainly (30) has a well-formed interpretation under which a nonovert subject in DP binds the reciprocal, where this nonovert subject can in turn corefer with the matrix subject. Of course, this interpretation, where the portraying is reciprocal rather than the admiring, is irrelevant here.

The relevant interpretation is the one under which the reciprocal is bound by the subject of the sentence, but not by the subject of the DP; in other words, the admiring is reciprocal, not the portraying. If we accept the judgments reported by Belletti (1982), then under this interpretation examples like (30) are ill formed. This cannot be predicted if the locality domain of *l'uno* is subject-based. Under a subject-based definition, if DP has no (accessible) subject, the locality domain for *l'uno* is clearly the sentence. Hence, binding of *l'uno* by the sentential subject is incorrectly predicted to be possible. Suppose then that we take the notion of barrier in (18) to define the locality domain for *l'uno*. DP is of course a barrier for *l'uno* under this definition. *L'uno* must then be construed with an antecedent inside DP. Since in sentences like (30) its relevant antecedent, the sentential subject, is DP-external, the sentence is correctly predicted to be ill formed under the relevant interpretation. Thus, the locality domain for *l'uno* must be defined by the notion of barrier in (18).

Another prediction that follows from the hypothesis that Italian reciprocals are associated with this definition of barrier, and does not follow from a subject-based definition, is that they cannot be found in DPs that are in subject position, unless again they are bound DP-internally. Thus, (31), where the only argument of N is bound DP-externally, is correctly predicted to be ungrammatical. On the other hand, given a definition of governing category based on the notion of accessible subject, the matrix sentence is the locality domain for the reciprocal in (31); and this incorrectly predicts that the reciprocal can be bound by the matrix subject.

(31) *Quei pittori$_i$ pensano che [gli ammiratori l'uno$_x$ dell'altro$_x$]
      those painters think   that the admirers   the one of the other
      siano detestabili
      are detestable

In short, Italian reciprocals support the conclusion that the barrier-type definition of locality is to be preferred to a subject-based definition of governing category for binding, as well as for movement. Still, remember that under the model of parameterization presented by Manzini and Wexler (1987), these two notions of locality need not be considered mutually exclusive, but can also be conceived of as alternative values of a parameter. According to this model, the definition of locality domain includes a multiple disjunction, which represents the locality parameter, each member of the disjunction identifying one of the values of this parameter. A markedness hierarchy is independently defined for the parameter by the Subset Principle, a learnability principle, on the basis of the subset relations among the languages generated by the different values of the parameter. The subject-based notion of governing category already represents one value of the parameter discussed by Manzini and Wexler (1987). The notion of barrier could then simply be added as another value.

According to the definition of markedness proposed by Manzini and Wexler (1987), the value of the locality parameter corresponding to the barrier-based notion of locality is less marked than the value corresponding to the subject-based notion, at least as far as anaphors are concerned. Indeed, the two notions are now defined in such a way that the subject-based one carries the same requirements as the barrier-based one, plus the additional requirement that it must contain a subject accessible to the element for which it is defined. It follows that all categories that are locality domains under the subject-based definition are also locality domains under the barrier-based definition, since the satisfaction of the former implies the satisfaction of the latter. But there will be some categories that are locality domains under the definition of barrier that are not locality domains under the subject-based definition, since this also requires the presence of an accessible subject.

If so, whenever an (antecedent, anaphor) link satisfies government (i.e., does not cross any barrier), it does not cross any subject-based locality domain either. However, an (antecedent, anaphor) link may cross a barrier and not cross a subject-based domain. Hence, all sentences that are grammatical under the definition of barrier in (18) are also grammatical under the subject-based definition of locality, but not vice versa. In other words, a grammar including the subject-based definition of locality generates a bigger language than a grammar including the definition of barrier in (18). Thus, if markedness hierarchies are defined in terms of the Subset Principle, the notion of barrier in (18) represents a less marked value of the locality parameter than the subject-based notion. Manzini and Wexler (1987) argue that the subject-based value of the locality parameter is unmarked with respect to all other values; since we have seen that it is marked with respect to the notion of barrier in (18), the latter now represents the unmarked value of the parameter.

Manzini and Wexler (1987), developing ideas proposed by Borer (1984), also hypothesize that a Lexical Parameterization Principle holds, to the effect that nondefault (i.e., marked) values of parameters can only be associated with lexical items; as a consequence, empty categories can only be associated with the default, or unmarked, value. If the unmarked value of the locality parameter corresponds to the definition of barrier in (18), we expect the latter to be associated with empty categories, hence with movement. This expectation is of course perfectly consistent with our findings. Technically, then, the definition of barrier in (18) and the subject-based definition can indeed be construed as values of the locality parameter, as conceived by Manzini and Wexler (1987).

If this line of thought is correct, then there is a unified, but parameterized, definition of locality. In particular, the values of the parameter correspond to the definition of barrier in (18), Chomsky's (1981) definition of governing category, and possibly other definitions. Since in its current formulation the definition of barrier forms part of the subject-based definition of locality, or in other words the subject-based definition of locality results from adding the notion of accessible subject to that of barrier, the parameterized definition of government can take the form in (32), essentially as suggested by Koster (1986). Under (32) the definition of barrier must invariably be satisfied; in addition, an accessible subject may be required, as well as other opacity elements.

(32) β is a locality domain for α iff

   0. β is a maximal projection, β dominates α (if α is g-marked, β dominates the g-marker of α), and

   1. β dominates a subject accessible to α

   2. ....

In summary, given a parameter of the type in (32), its obligatory part, corresponding to the notion of barrier, is its unmarked value; and this unmarked value is associated with movement, so that the locality theory for movement proposed here can be derived from (32). We would then expect that referentially dependent elements, whether anaphors or pronouns, can distribute themselves freely among the various values of the parameter. By the evidence presented so far, however, value 1 of the parameter in (32), corresponding to the subject-based notion of governing category, can and must be replaced by value 0, or the definition of barrier in (18). If so, the crucial question becomes whether the evidence in favor of other values of the parameter holds. If not, then (32) can and must be abandoned, and replaced again by a nonparameterized definition of locality, or barrier.

4.4 The Locality Parameter

The type of locality parameter presented by Manzini and Wexler (1987) as well as by previous authors, including Yang (1984), can be roughly characterized as ad hoc, in that differences in locality behavior are directly encoded in different definitions of locality domain. By contrast, a different type of parameter has emerged, associated in particular with the work of Pica (1987), which purports to account for the same data but is essentially non–ad hoc in its conception. According to Pica (1987), the locality parameter has, descriptively speaking, two values. One value is associated with anaphors such as English *himself*, the second value with anaphors such as Icelandic *sig*. Crucially, however, these two values do not correspond to a disjunction in the definition of locality domain of the type in (32). Rather, the different locality behaviors of *himself* and *sig* can be derived from a nonparameterized definition of locality, on the assumption that *himself* is a DP with a complex internal structure, but *sig* is a D/N head.

Consider Icelandic *sig*. (33)–(35) show that *sig* can be bound across an infinitival sentence boundary and across a subjunctive sentence boundary, but not across an indicative sentence boundary. On the other hand, (36)–(37) show that *sig* cannot be bound by a nonsubject across an infinitival or subjunctive sentence boundary; in the latter two cases *sig* must be bound by a subject, as in (33)–(34).

(33) Jón$_i$ skipaði Haraldi$_j$ að raka sig$_x$
      John ordered Harold   to shave SIG

(34) Jón$_i$ segir að María$_j$ elski sig$_x$
      John says that Mary love SIG

(35) Jón$_i$ segir að   María$_j$ elskar sig$_x$ i $\neq$ x
      John says that Mary loves SIG

(36) *Ég$_i$ lofaði   Jóni$_j$ að raka sig$_x$
      I   promised John to shave SIG

(37) Ég$_i$ sagði Jóni$_j$ að   María$_k$ hefði boðið sér$_x$ j $\neq$ x
      I   told John that Mary   had invited SIG

Apparently, neither of the behaviors in (33)–(37) follows from anything proposed so far. Indeed, under Manzini and Wexler's (1987) proposals, the behavior in (33)–(35) only follows from an additional value of the locality parameter in (32) under which the locality domain for *sig* is defined in terms of an (accessible) indicative I. As for the behavior in (36)–(37), it follows from an independent parameter under which *sig* is subject-oriented as opposed again to anaphors such as *himself* that can have both a subject and a nonsubject as an antecedent. The basic empirical problem of such a theory, however, where locality domain and choice of antecedent represent independent parameters, is that it predicts the existence of anaphors that are long-distance like *sig*, but are not subject-oriented like *himself*. Unfortunately, no such anaphors appear to exist.

On the other hand, suppose we assume with Pica (1987) that Icelandic *sig* differs from English *himself* in that, whereas *himself* is a DP with a complex internal structure, *sig* is a D/N head. In dealing with DP anaphors, we have seen that they cannot enter address-based dependencies, since they and their potential antecedents, which are also phrasal, have incompatible addresses. This limits DP anaphors to categorial index dependencies, and hence to local binding. Now suppose we assume that head anaphors differ from DP anaphors in that they can have head antecedents.

Consider the categorial index structure of (34), as in (38).

(38) Jón I$_i$ segir að María I$_j$ elski sig$_x$

Once the c-command constraint on sequences is taken into account, the only head that can possibly bind a head anaphor is I. Thus, I$_i$ and I$_j$ in (38) are possible antecedents for *sig*. However, long-distance binding by I$_i$ does not satisfy government, because at least a CP barrier is crossed. Hence, the long-distance reading of (34) cannot be derived under (38).

However, consider the address structure counterpart to (38). Suppose we take *sig* to be a D/N anaphor. We have seen that I can in principle serve as an antecedent for *sig*. But I can also form an address based sequence with the DP of which *sig* is a head, since I (i.e., Agr) is not itself addressed. Crucially, since such an address-based sequence can include any number of nonaddressed intermediate heads between *sig* and I, it will satisfy Locality. Thus, both long-distance binding of *sig* by the matrix I and short-distance binding by the embedded I are correctly predicted to arise, as in (39).

(39) Jón I$_i$ segir að María I$_k$ elski sig$_{x,(k,x)}$

Of course, since the long-distance reading of *sig* depends on the formation of an address-based sequence, and the formation of such a sequence in turn depends on I being the antecedent for *sig*, the relation between long-distance binding and subject orientation is ultimately derived.

Let us now compare this realization of Pica's (1987) main idea, which essentially follows the proposal in Manzini, to appear a, with Pica's own, original realization. According to the latter, anaphors move at LF. Because they are heads, anaphors such as *sig* undergo head-to-head movement; by contrast, DP anaphors such as *himself* undergo phrasal movement. The present treatment of head anaphors in terms of address-based sequences and Pica's (1987) treatment in terms of head-to-head movement straightforwardly translate into one another. Consider DP anaphors, however. If they move to $\bar{\text{A}}$-position, then they should be able to move long-distance in successive-cyclic fashion; if they move to A-position, then the question arises what A-position they move to, since none appears to be available. Furthermore, the question arises what forces DP anaphors to A-move, rather than $\bar{\text{A}}$-move; they must of course be forced to A-move if the correct locality behavior is to be derived. Locality theory cuts across all such difficulties. Anaphors need not move, at least as far as Locality theory is concerned, and the locality properties of DP anaphors reduce to the locality properties of A-movement (i.e., government), without any need for stipulation. Simply, neither DP anaphors nor A-traces can form address-based sequences, though for opposite reasons, so that the locality requirement for both reduces to antecedent government.

The only remaining empirical problem for Locality theory is paradoxically represented by sentences like (35), where *sig* cannot be bound long-distance across an indicative sentence boundary. The solution proposed by Pica (1987) again depends on head-to-head movement at LF. The idea is that an anaphor can pass through the C position of a subjunctive sentence, because this is deletable at LF. By contrast, the anaphor cannot pass through the C position of an indicative sentence because this is undeletable. Thus, a dependency formed across an indicative sentence is nonlocal, though a dependency formed across a subjunctive sentence is local. Unfortunately, a solution based on C deletability at LF is neither necessary nor sufficient within Locality theory. It is not necessary because in terms of this theory the C position can enter an address-based sequence with *sig* even if it is lexically realized, since it is addressless. It is not sufficient, because in order for the C position not to be able to enter an address-based sequence with *sig*, it is necessary for it to have an address of its own, and not simply to be realized.

Notice, however, that for the LF deletion solution to have some principled content, it is necessary to assume that the contrast in deletability between indicative and subjunctive C follows from the fact that some sort of LF content is associated with the former but not the latter. In fact, the only principled difference between indicatives and subjunctives appears to be, as proposed by Picallo (1984), that the Tense of subjunctives depends on a superordinate Tense, whereas the Tense of indicatives does not. In other words, only indicatives are truly tensed, and subjunctives are untensed. Thus, it appears that it is properties of Tense rather than of C that are at stake. Indeed, we can assume as before, that there is a T head that has Tense properties, and that these Tense properties differ between subjunctives and indicatives. In order to predict that *sig* can form an address-based dependency across a subjunctive, but not across an indicative, we need only assume that indicatives correspond to a +Tns head, subjunctives to a −Tns head. Remember, then, that we have independently argued with respect to the interaction of *wh*-islands and Tense that a +Tns head is addressed, so that (35) is associated with an addressed structure of the type in (40) (where α represents the position of *sig*).

(40)

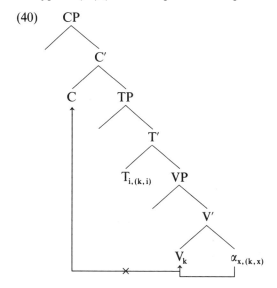

Given the structure in (40), the ill-formedness of (35) now follows. Indeed, in (40) no address-based sequence including α can include T because α and T have incompatible addresses; and an address-based link formed between C and V across T violates Locality. Hence, the inability of *sig* to be bound head-to-head across an indicative CP is correctly predicted. By contrast, head-to-head binding of *sig* across any number of $-$ Tns CPs is (again correctly) predicted to produce no violation. In turn, exactly as in the discussion of the interaction of Tense with *wh*-islands in chapter 2, given Chomsky's (1981) visibility requirement, all that is needed in order to derive that Tense must be addressed is the assumption that Tense is an argument. The argument role that Tense fills can be identified with the event role of V, in the sense of Higginbotham (1985), and the head that Case-marks or addresses it can be identified with V, through V-to-T incorporation. Since the mechanism for ruling out long-distance binding across Tense and the mechanism for predicting interactions of *wh*-islands with Tense are essentially the same, Locality theory effectively relates Tense effects on binding and movement, which remain at best separately explained under other theories.

Finally, just as there are long-distance subject-oriented anaphors, so there appear to be long-distance subject-oriented pronouns. For instance, the Icelandic pronoun *hann* must be disjoint in reference from a subject both in a simple sentence, as in (41), and across an infinitival sentence boundary, as in (42).

(41) Ég$_j$ lofaði   Jóni$_j$ að raka hann$_x$
      I   promised John to shave HANN

(42) *Jón$_i$ skipaði mér$_j$ að raka hann$_x$
      John ordered me   to shave HANN

Consider the crucial example in (42). If *hann* is taken to be a DP, then exactly the same predictions follow as for English *him*, namely, that *hann* can form a categorial index sequence but not an address-based sequence with any potential antecedent. Hence, *hann* must be disjoint in reference from the embedded subject, since it is governed by it, but not from the matrix subject. This is of course incorrect.

Suppose, however, that *hann* is taken to be a head. If so, like its anaphoric counterpart *sig*, we expect the DP of which it is a head to be able to form address-based sequences with both the embedded I and the matrix I in (42). Now, in the case of pronouns Locality effectively requires that no dependency that a pronoun forms with a given antecedent satisfies government. But the address-based dependencies that *hann* forms with the embedded and matrix I in (42) do satisfy government. Hence, coreference between *hann* and both the embedded and the matrix I is, correctly, ultimately blocked.

We may draw certain conclusions from this evidence. As originally observed by Pica (1987), the single most powerful argument in favor of a parameterized theory of locality—namely, the behavior of long-distance anaphors and pronouns such as those in Icelandic—is in fact only illusory. In particular, the behavior of long-distance anaphors and pronouns follows from a nonparameterized theory of locality if we assume that head dependencies of some sort, rather than phrasal dependencies, are involved in establishing their antecedents. Although Pica's (1987) original theory arguably suffered from a series of realization problems, the unified theory of locality developed here allows us to derive the correct results without need for any stipulation. It appears then that the strongest possible conclusion concerning locality is compatible with the available empirical evidence, namely, that there is a single locality principle and a single locality domain.

This result is obviously encouraging. First of all, Locality theory establishes the possibility of a locality component that is invariant across languages and across dependency types in a language, the wide apparent variation across languages and across dependencies being derived by random interaction of the various components of the grammar. This is precisely the kind of result that we expect under the principles-and-parameters model of Universal Grammar, which is therefore strengthened by it. In turn, the hypothesis on which Locality theory is based—namely, the existence of addresses and of address-based dependencies—makes a very powerful prediction regarding the existence of a twofold asymmetry between denotational and nondenotational elements: denotational elements are easy to move, but difficult to move across, and vice versa for nondenotational elements. To the extent that the data confirm this prediction, the specific form that Locality theory takes is also strongly supported.

References

Abney, S. (1987). "The English NP in Its Sentential Aspect." Doctoral dissertation, MIT.

Aoun, J. (1985). *A Grammar of Anaphora*. MIT Press, Cambridge, Mass.

Baker, M. (1988). *Incorporation*. University of Chicago Press, Chicago.

Belletti, A. (1982). "On the Anaphoric Status of the Reciprocal Construction in Italian." *The Linguistic Review* 2, 101–137.

Besten, H. den (1983). "On the Interaction of Root Transformations and Lexical Deletive Rules." In W. Abrahams, ed., *On the Formal Syntax of Westgermania*. John Benjamins, Amsterdam.

Borer, H. (1984). *Parametric Syntax*. Foris, Dordrecht.

Brody, M. (1982). "On Deletion and on Local Control." In A. Marantz and T. Stowell, eds., *MIT Working Papers in Linguistics* 4. Department of Linguistics and Philosophy, MIT.

Brody, M. (1985). "On the Complementary Distribution of Empty Categories." *Linguistic Inquiry* 16, 505–546.

Brody, M. (1990). "Some Remarks on the Focus Field in Hungarian." In J. Harris, ed., *UCL Working Papers in Linguistics* 2. Department of Linguistics, University College London.

Burzio, L. (1986). *Italian Syntax*. Kluwer, Dordrecht.

Chomsky, N. (1973). "Conditions on Transformations." In S. Anderson and P. Kiparsky, eds., *A Festschrift for Morris Halle*. Holt, Rinehart and Winston, New York.

Chomsky, N. (1981). *Lectures on Government and Binding*. Foris, Dordrecht.

Chomsky, N. (1982). *Some Concepts and Consequences of the Theory of Government and Binding*. MIT Press, Cambridge, Mass.

Chomsky, N. (1986a). *Barriers*. MIT Press, Cambridge, Mass.

Chomsky, N. (1986b). *Knowledge of Language*. Praeger, New York.

Chomsky, N. (1991). "Some Notes on Economy of Derivation and Representation." In R. Freidin, ed., *Principles and Parameters in Comparative Grammar*. MIT Press, Cambridge, Mass.

Cinque, G. (1980). "On Extraction from NP in Italian." *Journal of Italian Linguistics* 5, 47–99.

Cinque, G. (1991). *Types of A'-Dependencies*. MIT Press, Cambridge, Mass.

Dobrovie-Sorin, C. (1990). "Clitic Doubling, *Wh*-Movement, and Quantification in Romanian." *Linguistic Inquiry* 21, 351–397.

Dobrovie-Sorin, C. (to appear). *The Syntax of Romanian*. Foris, Dordrecht.

Emonds, J. (1978). "The Verbal Complex V'-V in French." *Linguistic Inquiry* 9, 151–175.

Frampton, J. (1990). "Parasitic Gaps and the Theory of *Wh*-Chains." *Linguistic Inquiry* 21, 49–78.

Frampton, J. (to appear a). "The Fine Structure of Wh-Movement and the Proper Formulation of the ECP." In W. Chao and G. Horrocks, eds., *Levels of Representation*. Foris, Dordrecht.

Frampton, J. (to appear b). "*Relativized Minimality*, A Review." *The Linguistic Review*.

Gazdar, G., E. Klein, G. Pullum, and I. Sag (1985). *Generalized Phrase Structure Grammar*, Basil Blackwell, Oxford.

Giorgi, A., and G. Longobardi (1990). *The Syntax of Noun Phrases*. Cambridge University Press, Cambridge.

Guéron, J. (1981). "Logical Operators, Complete Constituents, and Extraction Transformations." In R. May and J. Koster, eds., *Levels of Syntactic Representation*. Foris, Dordrecht.

Guéron, J., and T. Hoekstra (to appear). "Chaînes temporelles et phrases réduites." In H.-G. Obenauer, ed., *Structure de la phrase et théorie du liage*. Editions CNRS, Paris.

Hegarty, M. (1990). "On Adjunct Extraction from Complements." Ms., MIT.

Heim, I. (1987). "Where Does the Definiteness Restriction Apply?" In E. Reuland and A. ter Meulen, eds., *The Representation of (In)definiteness*. MIT Press, Cambridge, Mass.

Higginbotham, J. (1985). "On Semantics." *Linguistic Inquiry* 16, 547–593.

Huang, C.-T. J. (1982). "Logical Relations in Chinese and the Theory of Grammar." Doctoral dissertation, MIT.

Kayne, R. (1981a). "ECP Extensions." *Linguistic Inquiry* 12, 93–133. (Reprinted in Kayne 1984.)

Kayne, R. (1981b). "Unambiguous Paths." In R. May and J. Koster, eds., *Levels of Syntactic Representation*. Foris, Dordrecht. (Reprinted in Kayne 1984.)

Kayne, R. (1983). "Connectedness." *Linguistic Inquiry* 14, 223–249. (Reprinted in Kayne 1984.)

Kayne, R. (1984). *Connectedness and Binary Branching*. Foris, Dordrecht.

Kayne, R. (1989). "Null Subjects and Clitic Climbing." In O. Jaeggli and K. Safir, eds., *The Null Subject Parameter*, Kluwer, Dordrecht.

Koopman, H. (1984). *The Syntax of Verbs*. Foris, Dordrecht.

Koopman, H., and D. Sportiche (1990). "The Position of Subjects." Ms., UCLA.

Koster, J. (1978). *Locality Principles in Syntax*. Foris, Dordrecht.

Koster, J. (1986). *Domains and Dynasties*. Foris, Dordrecht.

Larson, R. (1988). "On the Double Object Construction." *Linguistic Inquiry* 19, 335–392.

Lasnik, H., and M. Saito (1984). "On the Nature of Proper Government." *Linguistic Inquiry* 15, 235–289.

Lasnik, H., and M. Saito (1992). *Move α*. MIT Press, Cambridge, Mass.

Lema, J., and M. L. Rivero (1990). "Long Head Movement: ECP vs. HMC." In *Proceedings of NELS 20*. GLSA, University of Massachusetts Amherst.

Longobardi, G. (1990). "Extraction from NP and the Proper Nature of Head Government." In Giorgi and Longobardi 1990.

Manzini, M. R. (1983). "Restructuring and Reanalysis." Doctoral dissertation, MIT.

Manzini, M. R. (1988). "Constituent Structure and Locality." In A. Cardinaletti, G. Cinque, and G. Giusti, eds., *Constituent Structure: Papers from the XI GLOW Conference. Annali di Ca' Foscari* and Foris, Dordrecht.

Manzini, M. R. (1990), "A New Formalization of Locality Theory for Movement." In J. Mascaró and M. Nespor, eds., *Grammar in Progress: GLOW Studies for H. van Riemsdijk*. Foris, Dordrecht.

Manzini, M. R. (1991a). "Locality and Parameters Again." In I. Roca, ed., *Logical Issues in Language Acquisition*. Foris, Dordrecht.

Manzini, M. R. (1991b). "Locality, Parameters and Some Issues in Italian Syntax." In J. Koster and E. Reuland, eds., *Long-Distance Anaphora*. Cambridge University Press, Cambridge.

Manzini, M. R. (1991c). "Parasitic Gaps and Locality Theory." Ms., University College London.

Manzini, M. R. (to appear a). "A Unification of Locality Theory for Movement and Binding." In H.-G. Obenauer, ed., *Structure de la phrase et théorie du liage*. Editions CNRS, Paris.

Manzini, M. R. (to appear b). "Locality Theory: Towards a Unification." In W. Chao and G. Horrocks, eds., *Levels of Representation*. Foris, Dordrecht.

References

Manzini, M. R., and K. Wexler (1987). "Binding Theory, Parameters and Learnability." *Linguistic Inquiry* 18, 413–444.

May, R. (1985). *Logical Form: Its Structure and Derivation.* MIT Press, Cambridge, Mass.

Melvold, J. (1986). "Factivity and Definiteness." Ms., MIT.

Milner, J.-C. (1985). *Ordres et raisons de langue.* Seuil, Paris.

Obenauer, H.-G. (1976). *Etudes de syntaxe interrogative du français.* Niemeyer, Tübingen.

Obenauer, H.-G. (1984). "On the Identification of Empty Categories." *The Linguistic Review* 4, 153–202.

Pesetsky, D. (1982). "Paths and Categories." Doctoral dissertation, MIT.

Pesetsky, D. (1987). "*Wh*-in Situ: Movement and Unselective Binding." In E. Reuland and A. ter Meulen, eds., *The Representation of (In)definiteness.* MIT Press, Cambridge, Mass.

Pica, P. (1987). "On the Nature of the Reflexivization Cycle." In *Proceedings of NELS 17.* GLSA, University of Massachusetts, Amherst.

Picallo, C. (1984). "Opaque Domains." Doctoral dissertation, CUNY, New York.

Pollock, J.-Y. (1989a). "Verb Movement, Universal Grammar, and the Structure of IP." *Linguistic Inquiry* 20, 365–424.

Pollock, J.-Y. (1989b). "Opacity, Genitive Subject and Extraction from NP in English and French." *Probus* 1, 151–162.

Reinhart, T. (1976). "The Syntactic Domain of Anaphora." Doctoral dissertation, MIT.

Reinhart, T., and E. Reuland (1991). "Anaphors and Logophors." In J. Koster and E. Reuland, eds., *Long-Distance Anaphora.* Cambridge University Press, Cambridge.

Rizzi, L. (1980). "Violations of the *Wh* Island Constraint and the Subjacency Condition." *Journal of Italian Linguistics* 5, 157–195. (Reprinted in Rizzi 1982.)

Rizzi, L. (1982). *Issues in Italian Syntax.* Foris, Dordrecht.

Rizzi, L. (1990). *Relativized Minimality.* MIT Press, Cambridge, Mass.

Rizzi, L. (1991). "Residual Verb Second and the Wh-Criterion." Ms., Université de Genève.

Roberts, I. (1991). "Head-Government and the Local Nature of Head-Movement." *GLOW Newsletter 26.*

Ross, J. R. (1967). "Constraints on Variables in Syntax." Doctoral dissertation, MIT.

Ross, J. R. (1984). "Inner Islands." In *Proceedings of BLS 10.* Berkeley Linguistic Society, University of California, Berkeley.

Rudin, C. (1988). "On Multiple Questions and Multiple Wh-Fronting." *Natural Language and Linguistic Theory* 6, 445–502.

Sportiche, D. (1988). "A Theory of Floating Quantifiers and Its Corollaries for Constituent Structure." *Linguistic Inquiry* 19, 425–449.

Stowell, T. (1981). "Origins of Phrase Structure." Doctoral dissertation, MIT.

Szabolcsi, A. (1991). "Islands, Monotonicity, Composition and Heads." *GLOW Newsletter* 26.

Szabolcsi, A., and F. Zwarts (1990). "Semantic Properties of Composed Functions and the Distribution of Wh-Phrases." In *Proceedings of the 7th Amsterdam Colloquium*. ILLC, University of Amsterdam.

Taraldsen, K. T. (1981). "On the Theoretical Interpretation of a Class of Marked Extractions." In A. Belletti, L. Brandi, and L. Rizzi, eds., *Theory of Markedness in Generative Grammar: Proceedings of the 1979 GLOW Conference*. Scuola Normale Superiore, Pisa.

Torrego, E. (1984). "On Inversion in Spanish and Some of Its Effects." *Linguistic Inquiry* 15, 103–129.

Travis, L. (1984). "Parameters and Effects of Word Order Variation." Doctoral dissertation, MIT.

Vergnaud, J.-R. (1985). *Dépendences et niveaux de représentation en syntaxe*. John Benjamins, Amsterdam.

Yang, D. W. (1984). "The Extended Binding Theory of Anaphors." *Language Research* 19, 169–192.

Index